The Quotable Cowboy

Other Books by Kathy Etling

Hunting Superbucks:
How to Find and Hunt
Today's Trophy Mule and Whitetail Deer

Cougar Attacks:
Encounters of the Worst Kind

Bear Attacks

The Quotable
Cowboy

EDITED AND WITH AN INTRODUCTION
BY KATHY ETLING

THE LYONS PRESS
Guilford, Connecticut
An imprint of The Globe Pequot Press

To
Shelby

Contents

Introduction xi

In the Beginning 1

The Code of the West 33

The Cowboy Way 49

Longhorns, Cow Ponies, and Mules 95

I Fought the Law 129

And They Call the Thing Rodeo 161

End of the Trail 181

Who's Who 205

Bibliography 233

Index 243

Introduction

No living thing was moving throughout that vast
landscape, except the lizards that darted over the
sand and through the rank grass and prickly pears at
our feet. . . . Before and behind us, the level
monotony of the plains was unbroken as far as the
eye could reach. Sometimes it glared in the sun, an
expanse of hot, bare sand; sometimes it was veiled by
coarse grass. Skulls and whitening bones of buffalo
were scattered everywhere.

—FRANCIS H. PARKMAN

One can only imagine the feelings that coursed through the
beings of those men who first explored this continent's inte-
rior. An endless sea of grass that had never felt cold steel,
creeks and rivers of unimagined purity snaking their way to

the sea, a sky so blue that it shimmered beneath the arc of the sun, all of this and more was beheld by those first explorers. They saw, but with unseeing eyes that constantly scanned the countryside for silver or gold or jewels, unaware of the treasures lying scattered like raw gemstones in every direction.

These first explorers, who had arrived here from Europe, had their day and departed, believing themselves to be failures. They had found no El Dorado, no Cibola, no beach littered with golden nuggets the size of a man's fist. The explorers came, they saw, and they left behind a few Spanish cattle, some runaway horses, and a land that must have seemed limitless, wild, mysterious, and all but unconquerable. The first explorers left without fully comprehending the riches they had found—riches that would define this new and unspoiled world.

The shifting winds of change gusted over North America, bringing on their currents another breed of human: the mountain man. Even more adventurous than earlier explorers, the wealth that these men sought was contained in the lush and silky pelage of beavers and foxes, muskrats, and wolves.

But the continent still slumbered, virtually untouched. Living conditions in even the mightiest cities left much to be desired. Many people survived with the crudest of implements, no running water, and no conveniences. Life was a drudgery of eking out the barest of necessities, including food. There was as yet no refrigeration and no canning. Many people lived rarely, if ever, tasting beef, a food item equated with power and wealth.

In the meantime, those first Spanish cattle, which would come to be known as Longhorns, flourished until great herds of the creatures roamed the Texas plains. Wild, mean, and intractable, Longhorns required special handling by special men. Thus was born the cattle drives: first to New Orleans, California, and Missouri, and later a two-year trek to New York. It wasn't until after the Civil War, however, that the real Age of the Cowboy began. When the able-bodied Texans who had been fighting the war returned, they found a depressed beef market due to the presence of so much beef on-the-hoof. Yet the northern markets, where cattle were scarce, beckoned. Men with vision looked to these markets and started out on the odyssey that has provided this country with our one enduring hero of mythical proportions: the cowboy.

"[They are] in appearance a species of centaur, half horse, half man, with immense rattling spurs, tanned skin, and dare-devil, almost ferocious faces," one traveler wrote of these range-toughened men who daily battled blistering heat or ferocious blizzards, driving rain or pelting hailstorms, prolonged drought or deadly stampedes to care for animals not their own for the then-princely sum of about $30 a month. They slept on the ground and had "a thousand things to eat: all of 'em beans," as one cook said. Many were as wild—and some as ferocious—as the Longhorns in their care. Each day, as they pushed their charges northward, the vast landscape was changing; the very earth was being resculpted by the trammeling of millions of Longhorn hooves traveling northward to the railroads at Abilene, Dodge City, and Newton, Kansas, or into Colorado, Wyoming, or Montana. Cowboys were often the trailblazers, following ancient routes whose names have become synonymous with the age and with America: the Goodnight-Loving, the Chisholm, the Texas, and the Dodge City trails, to name a few.

Towns flared into life when the herds, with their cowboys, made their appearances each summer. Dance halls and saloons hired "soiled doves" for the express purpose of catering to the cowboy in any number of ways, the better to separate him from his hard-earned drover's wages. Gambling was wide open and whiskey flowed like water, even if most of it was rotgut. Every cowboy carried a gun—sometimes several—and the resulting combination could be deadly. Fortified with false "courage," many a young cowboy who went north with a herd to earn money for his family now lies at rest in an unmarked grave on the outskirts of some Kansas town.

The Age of the Cowboy, according to historians, lasted about fourteen years. And yet everywhere today we can see the mark that he made upon this land: railroads that thrived when his herds filled the stock cars to move eastward, interstate highways that follow his old trails, towns that he founded and which told him to "move along" once civilization arrived, the small farms and ranches upon which he settled down to raise a herd of his own, and in modern modes of dress such as cowboy boots, hats, and bandannas. Modern Americans are a horse-owning society and many of us deck out our critters in tack that has come to us directly from cowboy innovators. Many words in our everyday usage owe their existence to the cowboy, even if a few of them came to us via his Spanish and Mexican *compadre*, the *vaquero*: dogie, Maverick, lariat, *remuda*, cavvy, dally, stampede, and chuckwagon, to name just a few.

The cowboys had feared the Native Americans, or "Indians," as they called them, but most lived to see the day when they would mourn their passing and the dearth of buffalo.

The cowboys were more diverse than TV shows and movies and even magazines seem to indicate. Fully twenty-five percent of them were black, many of whom had either fled slavery or were looking for a new start in life and seeking in out West. A good number were Hispanic, too. Women also contributed their share, although we will probably never know just how many women, disguised as a man, fled with the herds to escape an unadventurous life made up of little more than subservience and menial tasks.

There are some who would argue that the cowboy's age is with us yet. Indeed, when traveling across this great continent one need not get far from the beaten track to see evidence that the cowboy still reigns supreme. Many ranches employ cowboys because there is no handier, cheaper way to handle and care for cattle than with men or women who "know cow." Western music is experiencing a rebirth, as is western dancing. Western wear surges into vogue like clockwork every few seasons, but in many parts of the country dressing western isn't the choice of *fashionistas*, it is a requirement because it just makes sense.

Cowboys have influenced our popular culture through radio, TV, and films. They have been the focal point of slick ad campaigns because "cowboy sells." Rodeo and professional bull riding are both growing at phenomenal rates, and roughstock, roping, and barrel-racing schools are over-enrolled with wannabe rodeoers. Why?

Cowboys remind us of a time when life was simple, when everything was black and white, and when hope lay upon the horizon like a pale rising sun. The earliest drovers could not have foreseen this land we call America with all her boundless energy and wealth and food so plentiful we throw much of it away, and yet they are the ones who inspired much of it. We do something because it "is the cowboy way," we "cowboy up" to adversity, we "cowboy through" a difficult task. We are the heirs to their myth and to their legacy.

In short, we have mighty big boots to fill.

As you page through this book you will be struck by the difficulties these men faced and the "spin" they put upon their travails so that they might prevail. The older cowboys were like us in so many ways. They had to deal with low wages, sorry bosses, the occasional hangover, and the opposite sex. Today's rodeoers are, like many ordinary people, consumed with achieving stated goals, with winning, and ultimately prevailing. Ranchers, too, have been included here, although to a lesser extent, because today's rancher usually doesn't have the luxury of sitting back and taking it easy. He or she, instead, can often be found riding alongside the cowboys and involved in cowboy tasks. Like the cowboy, the rancher faces foes that are unrelenting: disease, weather, and cattle prices. But cowboy or rancher, through their lives runs a common theme: cowboy up.

Genres of fiction, film, and television have immortalized the cowboy, who has touched all corners of this great land, and he has influenced many different aspects of our lives. In this book, you will find his—and sometimes, her—wisdom, humor, insight, and downright foolishness. You will marvel at his courage and perseverance. You will examine his life and its travails in the context of our often-pampered existence. You will come to know the cowboy like you have never known him before, through the words that he has uttered or cared about enough that he wrote them down for posterity, as well as the words of scores of novelists, journalists, and historians. Once you have read this book, I think you will agree that the American cow-boy has touched other, intangible things as well: the hearts and the souls and the minds of we, the people, who admire him so.

Kathy Etling
May 2002

The Quotable Cowboy

1

In the Beginning

Everything in the West is life!

FREDERIC REMINGTON
The Denver Republican 1900

The West—the very words go straight to that place of the heart where Americans feel the spirit of pride in their western heritage—the triumph of personal courage over any obstacle, whether nature or man.

JOHN WAYNE (1907–1979)

The West, where a man can look farther and see less of anything but land and sky.

WILL JAMES (1892–1942)

It was a land of vast silent spaces, of lonely rivers, and of plains where the wild game stared at the passing horseman. It was a land of scattered ranches, of . . . long-horned cattle, and of reckless riders who unmoved looked in the eyes of life or of death.

THEODORE ROOSEVELT
An Autobiography (1913)

Of all the gifts that have come to me from contact with the West, this one of sheer love of wilderness, beauty, color, grandeur, has been the greatest, the most significant for my work.

> ZANE GREY, quoted in Zane Grey,
> *Romancing the West* (1997).

The west isn't a place that gives itself up easily.

> PAM HOUSTON
> "Cowboys are My Weakness"
> *Cowboys are My Weakness* (1992)

The history of every country begins in the heart of a man or a woman.

> WILLA CATHER
> *O Pioneers!* (1913)

The land of the heart is the land of the West.

GEORGE POPE MORRIS
"The West" (1838)

Out where the handclasp's a little stronger,
Out where the smile dwells a little longer,
That's where the West begins.

ARTHUR CHAPMAN
"Out Where the West Begins"
Out Where the West Begins (1917)

Go west, young man.

JOHN BABSON SOULE
Terre Haute Express 1851

I'll go back to the Western land,
I'll hunt up my old cowboy band,
Where the girls are few and the boys are true
and a false-hearted love I never knew.

From "The Trail to Mexico," Old Cowboy Song

It was a hard land, and it bred hard men to hard
ways.

LOUIS L'AMOUR (1908–1988)

We had the slickest horse thieves and nerviest rustlers, fastest running horses and rankest broncs, best riders and hard case fighting men in Montana . . . by God, it was absolutely so!

SPIKE VAN CLEVE
Forty Years' Gatherin's (1977)

Montana is still called the Land of the Shining Mountains.

BOB KENNON
From the Pecos to the Powder (1965)

I'd rather live in a place where I know somebody and everybody is Somebody.

CHARLES M. RUSSELL, discussing how he preferred Montana to New York City, quoted in *Charles Russell* (1989).

The town too tough to die!

COWBOY NAME FOR TUCSON, ARIZONA

———

Denver: the very name evokes the cowboy ideals of plain-spokenness and big shoulders.

CLAY BONNYMAN EVANS
I See by Your Outfit (1999)

———

The cowtown has a mystique all of its own. The word conjures up a vision of dusty streets, false fronted buildings, hitching posts, cattle pens, railroad tracks, and innumerable mounted cowboys.

JOSEPH G. ROSA
Age of the Gunfighter (1993)

Queen of the Cowtowns!

COWBOY NAME FOR DODGE CITY, KANSAS

Fort Worth is where the panther laid down and died.

C. H. Rust, describing a town so dull, he said a panther could sleep on its main street without being disturbed, quoted in *The Long Trail* (1976).

"Where do you want to go?" asked the conductor.
"To Hell," said the cowboy.
"Well, give me $2.50 and get off at Dodge."

Conversation overheard in Newton, Kansas, during the late 1800s, quoted in *Trail Driving Days* (1952).

Don't ever get the impression that you can ride your horses into a saloon, or shoot out the lights in Dodge.

MR. MCNULTA, quoted in *The Log of a Cowboy* (1903).

———•••———

Some people are malicious enough to think that if the devil were set at liberty and told to confine himself to Nevada Territory, he would . . . get homesick and go back to hell again.

MARK TWAIN (1835–1910)

If I owned Hell and Texas, I'd rent Texas and live in Hell.

> JIM FLOOD, about Texas weather, quoted in *The Log of a Cowboy* (1903).

Other states are carved or born;
Texas grew from hide and horn.

> BERTA HART NANCE (1883–1958)

The Texans are perhaps the best at the actual cow-boy work.

> THEODORE ROOSEVELT
> *Hunting Trips of a Ranchman* (1885)

You can always tell a Texan, but not much.

ANONYMOUS

———•+••◦———

One of the first things schoolchildren in Texas learn is how to compose a simple declarative sentence with the word *shit* in it.

ANONYMOUS

[I came to Texas] possessing only a horse, a saddle, and ten dollars in cash.

> RICHARD KING, 1846, founder of the vast King Ranch in Texas, quoted in *The Trail Drivers of Texas* (1925).

———

When H.C. Day founded the Lazy B Ranch in 1880, all the land was open range. There were no fences and no governing laws for the use of public lands. Anyone could put cattle on the land to graze.

> SANDRA DAY O'CONNOR
> *Lazy B* (2002)

I'm Dusty, my wife is Sandy, my boy is Rocky, and my daughter's name is Wendy. Our names describe this ranch perfectly.

DUSTY RAY, quoted in *The Cowboy Kind* (2001).

———●•••●———

Many ranches had unbroken family ownership into the third, fourth, and fifth generation. It conveyed, in a peculiar way, a sort of immortality to those who had gone on.

ELMER KELTON
"Continuity" (1995)

Oh give me a home where the buffalo roam,
And the deer and the antelope play,
Where seldom is heard a discouraging word,
And the skies are not cloudy all day.

BREWSTER HIGLEY
"Home on the Range" (1873)

He'd like the raw life of the camp . . . he missed the rough company and the unpredictable nature of a place that could double its population almost overnight once a major lode was uncovered, or lose a citizen in a heartbeat when the same card turned up twice in a poker game in one of the tents.

LOREN D. ESTELMAN
"The Cat King of Cochise County" (1995)

When the northern trails became an institution the Texan was trail-boss and straw-boss; and as boss he was a dictator.

EDWARD DOUGLAS BRANCH
The Cowboy and His Interpreters (1926)

Nowhere . . . does a man feel more lonely than when riding over the far-reaching, seemingly never-ending plains.

THEODORE ROOSEVELT
Hunting Trips of a Ranchman (1885)

Above all things, the plainsmen had to have an instinct for direction. I never had a compass in my life, but I was never lost.

CHARLES GOODNIGHT (1836–1929)

Any cowboy who knows his trails can start from the Canadian border and ride all the way to Mexico without hitting a fence [in] . . . 1940.

> WILL JAMES
> *The American Cowboy* (1942)

———•·••·•———

By 1869, the main trails were well defined. . . . The best known of these was the Chisholm Trail . . . [which] ran north from Red River Station across the Indian Territory, and entered Kansas near Caldwell. It crossed the Arkansas River at Wichita and continued past the present site of Newton to Abilene.

> FLOYD B. STREETER
> *Prairie Trails and Cow Towns* (1936)

It was there in the shadow of the mountains the cowboy disease first infected me, there where I found a preference for the sky as my ceiling and felt first yearnings for independence and self-sufficiency.

CLAY BONNYMAN EVANS
I See by Your Outfit (1999)

I sat on my horse every night while we were crossing through the Indian country. I was so afraid, I could not sleep in the tent.

> TOM PONTING, 1853, quoted in *The Canadian Cowboy* (1993).

———

In the year 1845, he left home and went out West, far beyond the country's creeping frontier, where he hoped to find his equals. He had the idea that in Indian country, where there was danger, all white men were kings, and he wanted to be one of them.

> DOROTHY M. JOHNSON
> "A Man Called Horse" (1949)

We stole every inch of land we got from the Injun but we didn't get it without a fight, and Uncle Sam will remember a long time.

CHARLES M. RUSSELL
Trails Plowed Under (1927)

The cowboys called it "No Man's Land."

L. D. TAYLOR in 1869, talking about Indian Territory (present day Oklahoma), quoted in *The Trail Drivers of Texas* (1925).

Reality showed me desolate mountains gleaming bare in the sun, long lines of red bluffs, white sand dunes . . . fading all around into the purple haze of the deceiving distance.

ZANE GREY, quoted in *Zane Grey, Romancing the West* (1997).

Mounted on my favorite horse, my . . . lariat near my hand, and my trusty guns in my belt . . . I felt I could defy the world.

Nat Love
The Life and Adventures of Nat Love (1907)

When I was young, I fell in love with horses, the cowboy lifestyle and Western music, and it set the course for my whole life.

MICHAEL MARTIN MURPHEY

———

Every American child should learn at school the history of the conquest of the West. The names Kit Carson, of General Custer and of Colonel Cody should be as household words. . . . Nor should Sitting Bull, the Short Wolf, Crazy Horse . . . be forgotten. They too were Americans, and showed the same heroic qualities as did their conquerors.

R. B. CUNNINGHAME GRAHAM in a letter to Theodore Roosevelt (1917).

They hunted buffalo and lived in the open, away from settled places. That sort of life tended to keep a man fit.

JOHN JAKES
The Lawless (1978)

The vaquero thought so much of his *reata* (lariat) that he wouldn't let it touch the ground if he could help it.

WILL JAMES
The American Cowboy (1942)

Does it blow like this all the time? Hell, no! Blows the other way half the time.

Anonymous cowboy remarking on the prairie wind.

God willing and the creek don't rise.

Spoken by any cowboy—or westerner—familiar with the fickle nature of the region's creeks and rivers.

All signs fail in dry weather.

Old cowboy saying that means how nothing can predict rain during a drought.

You have to chew it before you can swallow it.

Old cowboy saying about muddy drinking water.

On the range, the supply of good cooks was always low and the demand keen.

RAMON F. ADAMS (1889–1976)

The grub pile

Cowboy's way of referring to a meal or chuckwagon.

Pecos strawberries

Drover slang for beans.

Sonofabitch stew

Cowboy concoction containing cow heart, testicles, tongue, liver, and marrow gut, and probably first served on a trail drive using ingredients at hand.

This dern grits is burned, but that's the way I like it.

BONE MIZELL, thinking quickly to avoid violating the rule that a cow hunter was not allowed to complain about the food served on roundups, quoted in the Florida Cow Hunter (1990).

Come and get it or I'll throw it in the creek.

How chuckwagon cooks woke the trail drivers.

———

Here's the Cowboy's recipe for coffee: Take one pound of coffee, wet it good with water, boil it for thirty minutes, pitch a horse shoe in and, if it sinks, put in some more coffee.

A Treasury of Western Folklore (1975)

———

Treat a mad rattlesnake and a chuckwagon cook alike: Don't mess with either one.

R. LEWIS BOWMAN
Bumfuzzled (1992)

My ceiling's the sky, my floor is the grass,
My music's the lowing of herds as they pass.
My books are the brooks, my sermons the stones,
My parson's a wolf on his pulpit of bones.

OLD COWBOY SONG

My seat in the saddle, saddle in the sky,
I'll quit punchin' cows in the sweet bye and bye.

"The Old Chisholm Trail," an old drover song.

2

The Code of the West

A man's got to have a code, a creed to live by, no matter his job.

JOHN WAYNE (1907–1979)

————•◦•◦•————

The Code of the West was a gentleman's agreement to certain rules of conduct. It was never written into the statutes, but it was respected everywhere on the range.

RAMON F. ADAMS (1889–1976)

Take care of your horse before you take care of yourself.

THE CODE OF THE WEST

A horse thief pays with his life for stealing a horse.

THE CODE OF THE WEST

Don't mount another man's horse, and never try on his hat.

THE CODE OF THE WEST

The Code of her West: Use a short rope, a sweet smile, and a hot brand.

GLADIOLA MONTANA
Never Ask a Man the Size of his Spread (1993)

Ride!

THE COWBOY'S PHILOSOPHY

———•••••———

A cowboy never asks another cowboy about his past.

THE COWBOY'S CODE

———•••••———

A closed mouth gathers no boots.

OLD COWBOY SAYING

———•••••———

Speak yer mind, but ride a fast horse.

TEXAS BIX BENDER
Don't Squat with Yer Spurs On (1992)

Cowboys call no man master.

THEODORE ROOSEVELT (1858–1919)

A cowboy is kind to children, old folks and animals.

GENE AUTRY (1907–1998)

Never pass anyone on the trail without saying "Howdy."

THE COWBOY'S CODE

I believe that everyone has within himself the power to make this a better world.

FROM THE "THE LONE RANGER'S CREED"

The values of the cowboy are solid—belief in God, belief in country, belief in family.

CHRIS ISAACS
American Cowboy January/February 2000

When you travel by pack train you get a whole new perception of the goodness of people.

TOM DAVIS
Be Tough or Be Gone (1984)

I wish I could find words to express the trueness, the bravery, the hardihood, the sense of honor, the loyalty to their trust and to each other of the old trail hands.

CHARLES GOODNIGHT, quoted in *Charles Goodnight* (1949).

One of the main characteristics of the cowboy is loyalty.

Texas Livestock Journal 1882

You can gripe and complain amongst yourselves, but God help the outsider who cusses the brand.

RED STEAGULL
Ride for the Brand (2000)

Cuss all you want . . . but only around men, horses, and cows.

OLD COWBOY SAYING

Only quitters complain, and cowboys hate quitters.

OLD COWBOY SAYING

For three decades, and perhaps longer, the drift [in America] has been . . . a downward spiral into blame, finger-pointing, pessimism, self-pity, and litigiousness. It's been a slide into a culture of whining and rationalizing. . . . It hasn't been classic American can-do-ism. And it ain't been cowboy, either.

JESSE MULLINS
American Cowboy September/October 2000

Virtue is its own punishment.

OLD COWBOY SAYING

Always keep your word; a gentleman never insults anyone intentionally; and don't look for trouble, but if you get into a fight, make sure you win it.

> JOHN WAYNE, words from his father by which he lived his life, quoted in *John Wayne: There Rode a Legend* (2000).

Whenever there is [trouble], we'll depend on ourselves. We'll take care of it—when it comes, not after it's too late.

WILL JAMES
The American Cowboy (1942)

You'll never break a horse if you stay sittin' on the fence.

OLD COWBOY SAYING

A cowboy will not submit tamely to an insult.

THEODORE ROOSEVELT
Ranch Life and the Hunting-Trail (1888)

A cowboy never takes unfair advantage—even of an enemy.

GENE AUTRY (1907–1998)

Cowards never lasted long enough to become real cowboys.

CHARLES GOODNIGHT (1836–1929)

[Courage] comes from taking everything life hands you and being your best either because of it or in spite of it.

TY MURRAY
American Cowboy September/October 2000

Cowboys are heroic because they exercise human courage on a daily basis.

John Erickson, quoted in *Ranching Traditions* (1989).

For a bullfighter, heart—sometimes called courage— is the most important job qualification of all.

Dwayne Hargo, quoted in *Rodeo in America* (1996).

Cowboy up!

Rodeo call; also means to go on, no matter what, injured or healthy.

No cowboy ever quit while his life was hardest and his duties were most exacting.

J. FRANK DOBIE
A Vaquero of the Brush Country (1929)

A job doesn't get done when it's started with a promise and finished with an alibi.

R. Lewis Bowman
Bumfuzzled Too (2001)

———•••———

You've got to get the job done, whatever it takes—
that's the cowboy way.

Cody Lambert, quoted in *Gold Buckle* (1995).

3

The Cowboy Way

A cowboy is a man with guts and a horse.

WILL JAMES (1892–1942)

———•••••———

Working cowboys are the embodiment of the true American spirit.

CLINT EASTWOOD, in the Foreword to *Gathering Remnants* (2001).

There's something old-fashioned about cowboys, but then there's something old-fashioned about the Fourth of July, and rodeo, and backyard barbecues with friends.

JESSE MULLINS
American Cowboy July/August 2001

Fighting his way with knife and gun, the Texas cowboy was evolved, a fearless rider, a workman of sublime self-confidence, unequaled in the technique and tricks of cowpunching, the most accurate on the trigger and the last to leave untasted the glass which the bartender silently refilled.

EDWARD DOUGLAS BRANCH
The Cowboy and His Interpreters (1926)

Cowpunchers were . . . all careless, homeless, hard-drinking men.

CHARLES M. RUSSELL
Trails Plowed Under (1927)

Us cowboys wasn't respectable, but then again we didnt pretend to be.

E. C."TEDDY BLUE"ABBOTT
We Pointed Them North (1939)

Sinewy, hardy, self-reliant, their life forces them to be both daring and adventurous, and the passing over their heads of a few years leaves printed on their faces certain lines which tell of dangers quietly fronted and hardships uncomplainingly endured.

THEODORE ROOSEVELT
Hunting Trips of a Ranchman (1885)

A cowboy is a common laborer with heroic tendencies and a sense of humor, who lives with animals.

JOHN R. ERICKSON, quoted in *Ranching Traditions* (1989).

The men that knew cow.

OLD PHRASE MEANING "COWBOYS" OR "DROVERS."

It's grand, really grand, to be a cowboy and alone in the woods, punching a wild cow off through the brush, yelling and spurring.

RALPH REYNOLDS
Growing Up Cowboy (1991)

The cowboys rode half-wild horses, worked with wild cattle, and were themselves far from tame.

ANDY RUSSELL
The Canadian Cowboy (1993)

Cowboys are often inattentive to instructions, inefficient in their methods of travel, and seldom ruled by schedules, but they possess a dogged narrow-mindedness when in pursuit of a good time.

BAXTER BLACK
Cactus Tracks and Cowboy Philosophy (1997)

They were cowboys, I think, but there wasn't anything romantic or wonderful about them. They were rough-looking men with heavy gauntlets stuck behind their belts and big pistols hanging in pouches at their waists.

FRANK RODERUS
"I Never Saw a Buffalo" (2000)

Keep them out where the winds blow, the sands storm and the animals resist all reasonable effort and they remain superb workmen, alert, humorous, and subtle.

LARRY MCMURTRY (1936–)

Cowboys are as different as the stars and sky.

KURT MARKUS
American Cowboy January/February 2001

The cowman is never able to pay a good cowboy what he's worth. On the other hand, a sorry one is always overpaid.

R. Lewis Bowman
Bumfuzzled (1992)

———•·•·•———

Age and size . . . got nothin' to do with it. You gotta want to be a cowboy, keep your eyes open and your mouth shut and . . . don't think you know it all the first year.

Pat Hughes, quoted in *Hashknife Cowboy* (1984).

———•·•·•———

Son, if you want to ensure that you'll always be able to eat, learn to ride a colt and shoe a horse.

Buck Brannaman
The Faraway Horses (2001)

Cowboys of Luna Kid's generation had . . . learned to use an axe, a crowbar, and a pitchfork. They could take a rasp and pinchers and shoe a horse, knock over a buck at 200 yards with a .30-30, tend a thresher, and doctor a cow.

RALPH REYNOLDS discussing cowboys who came of age during World War II.
Growing Up Cowboy (1991)

I learned a bunch from the old guys.

MIKE MILLER
American Cowboy July/August 2000

You never saw an old cowpuncher.
They were scarce as hen's teeth.
Where they went to, heaven only knows.

JOHN RANDOLPH CLAY
My Life on the Range (1924)

Hell, I been cowboyin' all my life and I'm still learnin'.

PAT HUGHES, quoted in *The Hashknife Cowboy* (1984).

[I have known cowpunchers] who could neither read nor write, but who could name any brand . . . on a cow.

EVANS COLEMAN, quoted in *The Cowboys* (1973).

I was raising horses when I was raising my children. I raised them together. I credit that relationship with the fact that not one of my children has ever been involved with drugs.

REX ALLEN, quoted in *The Cowboy Kind* (2001).

The cowboy goes to the school of nature.

WILL JAMES (1892–1942)

If I hadn't have been a cowpuncher, I never could have growed up.

E. C. "TEDDY BLUE" ABBOTT, explaining how a doctor had advised him to stay out in the open air. *We Pointed Them North* (1939)

My advice to any young man or boy is to stay at home and not be a rambler. . . . And above everything stay away from a cow ranch.

JAMES EMMIT MCCAULEY
A Stove-Up Cowboy's Story (1965)

I still wore Pampers under my Wranglers when I started my riding career at age 2.

TY MURRAY
Roughstock (2001)

I put a rope in Guy's hand before he could walk, and he's been carrying it . . . ever since.

JAMES ALLEN referring to his son, Guy "The Legend" Allen, a 16-time world steer-roping champion.
American Cowboy September/October 2000

I was riding alone when most kids were being told fairy tales.

BOB KENNON
From the Pecos to the Powder (1965)

They find themselves raising him the cowboy way and figure that's better than any other way.

J. P. S. BROWN
American Western Magazine October 2001

I growed three inches and gained ten pounds that night.

> E. C. "TEDDY BLUE" ABBOTT, age fourteen in 1875, upon hearing the trail boss say, "In a year or two Teddy will be a real cowboy."
> *We Pointed Them North* (1939)

When you use the term "cowboy," . . . you have to be careful. . . . We've had Hollywood cowboys and rodeo cowboys, rhinestone cowboys and Coca-cola cowboys, urban cowboys and midnight cowboys, Marlboro cowboys and Dallas cowboys.

> JOHN R. ERICKSON, quoted in *Ranching Traditions* (1989).

It is easier to get an actor to be a cowboy than to get a cowboy to be an actor.

> JOHN FORD (1894–1973)

I'm a better cowboy than an actor.

BRUCE BOXLEITNER (1950–)

I'm not a cowboy by any stretch of the imagination, in the real world, but I don't think there are a lot of guys in the acting business that have more affinity for that way of life than I do.

SAM ELLIOTT
American Western Magazine October 2001

The old-time movie cowboys shaped my body and mind for all the years to come after.

RONALD REAGAN (1911–)

I tried to make the western hero a roughneck.

JOHN WAYNE (1907–1979)

Westerns were to movies what the sports page is to the daily newspaper: the best part of it.

GENE AUTRY (1907–1998)

[A western] is that fantasy of a guy solving a problem himself. He doesn't dial 911. He works out the situation himself. If he doesn't, he doesn't exist.

CLINT EASTWOOD (1930–)

Hi, my name is John Ford and I make westerns.

JOHN FORD (1894–1973), legendary director of western movies would always introduce himself in this manner despite making movies in many different genres.

———

Trying to single out one of my pictures is like trying to single out a particular noodle you enjoyed in a spaghetti dinner.

GENE AUTRY (1907–1998)

———

I never smoked a cigarette in a picture. And I never entered a saloon except to deal justice to an outlaw.

TOM MIX (1880–1940)

Television put the cowboy into every American home.

ALBERT MARRIN
Cowboys, Indians and Gunfighters (1993)

Nobody watches TV westerns more avidly than . . . cowboys.

LARRY MCMURTRY (1936–)

We didn't have electricity and that meant we didn't have TV. We had darn poor radio too. So that meant we did the strangest things at night . . . we talked to each other!

WADDIE MITCHELL

People like westerns because they always know who's gonna win.

HOOT GIBSON (1892–1962)

I ride into a place owning my horse, saddle and bridle. It isn't my quarrel, but I get into trouble doing the right thing for somebody else. When it's all ironed out, I never get any money reward.

TOM MIX (1880–1940)

The Western is about moving on.

THOMAS MCGUANE

I put in eighteen or twenty years on the trail, and all I had in the [end] was the high-heeled boots, the striped pants and about $4.80 worth of other clothes, so there you are.

G. D. Burrows, quoted in *The Trail Drivers of Texas* (1925).

I spent two or three months' wages for an outfit, spurs, etc., trying to make myself look like a thoroughbred Cow Boy from Bitter Creek.

Charles Siringo
A Texas Cowboy (1888)

Dressin' a cowboy in formal attire is like puttin' earrings on a pig.

> R. LEWIS BOWMAN
> *Bumfuzzled* (1992)

A man's not a man without a Stetson.

> "PUT" PUTNEY, Texas Ranger, quoted in *Guns and the Gunfighters* (1975).

He's all hat and no cattle.

> OLD COWBOY SLUR.

It only takes a couple of good summer rains to make a cowman think he's on the high dollar end of society.

R. LEWIS BOWMAN
Bumfuzzled, Too (2001)

They had on about four dollars' worth of clothes between them, and rode McClellan saddles, with saddle bags, and guns tied on before.

FREDERIC REMINGTON
"Cracker Cowboys of Florida"
Harpers New Monthly Magazine August 1895

From [the cowboy's] wide-brimmed hat to his spurs and boots, he was different, and every item of his equipment—saddle, bridle, lariat, quirt, and guns—was designed [for] his kind of work.

ANDY RUSSELL
The Canadian Cowboy (1993)

Cowboys have worked the style angle well and long and have now . . . got it down good.

KURT MARKUS
American Cowboy January/February 2001

It's very hip to be a cowboy now, but in the '40's, cowboys were the bottom of the social scale.

IAN TYSON
Western Styles August 1995

There is something romantic about him. He lives on horseback, as do the Bedouins; he fights on horseback, as did the knights of chivalry; he goes armed with a strange new weapon which he uses ambidextrously and precisely; he swears like a trooper, drinks like a fish, wears clothes like an actor, and fights like a devil . . . He is a cowboy, a typical Westerner.

WALTER PRESCOTT WEBB
The Great Plains (1931)

Perhaps in no other occupation of men was the theory of the "survival of the fittest" more plainly demonstrated . . . than in the quick weeding out of the weakling, of the visionary, and of the inherently depraved, among those who understood the cowboy life.

ANONYMOUS

The cowboys have language intelligible only to the initiated. They call a horse herder a "horse wrangler," and a horse-breaker a "bronco buster." Their steed is often a "cayuse," and to dress well is to "rag proper." When a cowboy goes out on the prairie he "hits the flat." Whiskey is "family disturbance," and to eat is to "chew." His hat is a "cady," his whip a "quirt," his rubber coat a "slicker," his leather overalls are "chaps," or "chapperals," and his revolver is a ".45." Bacon is "overland trout," and unbranded cattle are "mavericks."

Finney County Democrat 26 March 1887

Residents knew bunkhouses by various names: "doghouses," "shacks," "dumps," "dives," and "louse cages."

ALBERT MARRIN
Cowboys, Indians and Gunfighters (1993)

You know a cowboy by the way he stands and walks and talks.

E. C. "TEDDY BLUE" ABBOTT
We Pointed Them North (1939)

———

The stranger's slow approach might have been a mere leisurely manner of gait or the cramped short steps of a rider unused to walking; yet, as well, it could have been the guarded advance of one who took no chances with men.

ZANE GREY
Riders of the Purple Sage (1912)

There goes the bravest man in the world. He wears that blamed white suit every day of the year and chews tobacco.

REX ALLEN TO CHRISTIAN "BUDDY" EBSEN discussing Herb Yates of Republic Pictures.
American Cowboy March/April 2000

It sure is true that there's more cowboys than rich people.

ANONYMOUS

During all my [cowpunchin'] experience in the Montana country I never knew a cowboy who could or would yodel.

D. J. O'MALLEY
Reminiscences and Poems of Early Montana and the Cattle Range (1934)

Y'know, I was the first singing cowboy. But there were three of us. The guy playin' the guitar, the fella singin', and me. We three were the first singin' cowboy!

JOHN WAYNE, quoted in *John Wayne: There Rode a Legend* (2000).

I rode bulls and horses for two years . . . but I got tired of pickin' myself up off the arena floor. I found a guitar never kicked me, never hurt me a bit, so I decided [to] stick with that.

REX ALLEN
American Cowboy March/April 2000

He enjoyed riding and dancing better than anyone I ever knew, and over-indulgence in the two exercises cause an abscess to form on his liver which called him hence in 1876.

BRANCH ISABELL, quoted in *The Trail Drivers of Texas* (1925).

Cowboys don't worry what people think of their musical tastes.

JESSE MULLINS
American Cowboy July/August 2001

Them brutes don't have no ear for music.

RAMON F. ADAMS (1889–1976), quoting what an old cowboy told ANDY ADAMS about singing to cattle.

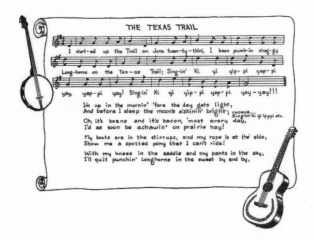

Kid, you are fired. I thought you told me you could sing. It's a hell of a note that cattle can't stand your singing.

AB BLOCKER, trail boss, quoted in *The Kaw* (1941).

If you got to talking to most cowboys, they'd admit they write 'em. I think some of the meanest, toughest sons of bitches around write poetry.

Ross Knox, quoted in Michael Riley "In Arizona: Cowboy Poets" *Time* 25 November 1985

———

There is charm about a man who is wild. Don't fall for it.

Gladiola Montana
Never Ask a Man the Size of his Spread (1993)

———

Don't you wed with those Texas boys.

Song of the late 1800s warning girls about cowboys

I've always had this thing for cowboys, maybe because I was born in New Jersey. But a real cowboy is hard to find these days, even in the West.

PAM HOUSTON
"Cowboys are My Weakness," *Cowboys are My Weakness* (1992).

I'm sittin' her.

COWBOY TALK FOR COURTING DURING THE DROVER DAYS.

A steady old mare is more reliable than a high-steppin' filly.

PARRY BEASLEY
1996 Conversation

Before you get serious about a cowboy, make sure he values you more than his truck.

GLADIOLA MONTANA
Never Ask a Man the Size of his Spread (1993)

A woman can go farther with a lipstick than a man with a Winchester and a side of bacon.

CHARLES M. RUSSELL
Trails Plowed Under (1927)

In summer, most of my cowboys are girls.

VAN IRVINE, on the difficulties in finding enough young men to fill his cowboy jobs during the 1960s and 1970s, quoted in *The American Cowboy in Life and Legend* (1972).

Dangers lurked on every hand, but bravely and uncomplainingly these women endured their hard lot, cheering and encouraging the men who were their protectors. God bless them!

GEORGE W. SAUNDERS, quoted in *The Long Trail* (1976).

I . . . hate namby-pamby heroines who just stand around while men do violent and admirable things.

DALE EVANS (1912–2001)

[The West] was a land where women were strong.

AGNES SMEDLEY, quoted in *The Real American Cowboy* (1985).

I was considered the most reckless and daring rider and one of the best shots in the western country.

> CALAMITY JANE
> *Life and Adventures of Calamity Jane, by Herself*

Albert, you stay outside. You're too young to come in here.

> CALAMITY JANE, to her young husband, outside a Montana saloon, quoted in *Forty Years' Gatherin's* (1977).

Little Sure Shot

> SITTING BULL'S nickname for ANNIE OAKLEY.

Cowboys didn't know anything about the fair sex and they used to blush as red as a turkey gobbler's neck when a girl would put her hand on one of their arms to walk off the dance floor.

SHINE PHILIPS
Big Spring (1942)

They get bored real quick. The way of life and the pace of life is too low-key.

MIKE MILLER explaining how most big city girls are unable to adapt to ranch life.
American Cowboy September/October 2000

A ranch woman has a lot in common with a prisoner in solitary confinement. She is often starved for conversation.

BAXTER BLACK
Cactus Tracks and Cowboy Philosophy (1992)

[His face] had all the characteristics of the range rider's—the leanness, the red burn of the sun, and the set changelessness that came from years of silence and solitude.

ZANE GREY
Riders of the Purple Sage (1912)

The hills git awful quiet, when you have to camp alone.

BRUCE KISKADDON (1878–1950)

In a place of all-encompassing silence, any sound is something to be noted and remembered.

SANDRA DAY O'CONNOR
Lazy B (2002)

I have gone for weeks at a time without seeing a soul.

JIM CHRISTIAN, quoted in *The Cowboys*, 1973.

In the city men shake hands and call each other friends but its the lonsome places that ties their harts together.

CHARLES M. RUSSELL, in a letter to Tom Conway,
24 March 1917
Charlie Russell Journal (1997)

Hi, lonesome!

COWBOY GREETING ANOTHER COWBOY

250 miles to the nearest post office
100 miles to wood
20 miles to water
6 inches to hell
God bless our home
Gone to live with the wife's folks

SIGN ON A PRAIRIE CABIN DOOR

The range life was not one calculated to make men soft.

LOUIS L'AMOUR
The Rustlers of West Fork (1951)

The day is never long enough, the week is always too short.

JOHN R. ERICKSON
LZ Cowboy (1996)

The cowboy . . . exists in enviable surroundings tempered by the sounds of nature and silence. They know true freedom: freedom from cell phones and traffic, and bound only by the vast horizon and some four-legged friends.

CLINT EASTWOOD in the Foreword to *Gathering Remnants* (2001).

Who ever heard of a cowboy with ulcers?

RAMON F. ADAMS (1889–1976)

Nobody ever saw a cowboy on the psychiatrist's couch.

JOHN WAYNE (1907–1979)

We don't have knights or kings or gurus in our tradition. . . . We come from cowboys, and that's who we are, for better or worse.

JOHN ERICKSON, quoted in *Ranching Traditions* (1989).

The great cowboys are the ones with the biggest hearts.

TY MURRAY
Roughstock (2001)

Cowboys are heroes, but not of the Hollywood variety. Their heroism comes in small portions. John Wayne may have saved the stampeding herd in Red River, but in real life the herd is saved one calf at a time.

DAVID MCCUMBER
The Cowboy Way (2000)

Most anything you want to say about cowboys is true. But the important thing is, they take care of cows.

CASWELL MCDOWELL, quoted in *The American Cowboy in Life and Legend* (1972).

4

Longhorns, Cow Ponies, and Mules

A man afoot is no man at all.

OLD COWBOY SAYING

A man afoot is useless.

JIM FLOOD, quoted in *Log of a Cowboy* (1903).

Cowboys are lucky that God invented the horse. Handling range cows would be . . . far more difficult . . . on foot.

BAXTER BLACK, quoted in *Ranching Traditions* (1989).

———

There were only two things the old-time cowpunchers were afraid of: a decent woman and being set afoot.

E. C. "TEDDY BLUE" ABBOTT (1860–1939)

———

[The cowboy] don't need no iron hoss, but covers his country on one that eats grass and wears hair.

CHARLES M. RUSSELL (1864–1926)

No other relationship between humans and animals is as close as when one is riding a horse.

SANDRA DAY O'CONNOR
Lazy B (2002)

Nothing does more for the inside of a man than the outside of a horse.

WILL ROGERS (1879–1935)

God's greatest gift to the man is the horse.

JOHN GROWNEY, quoted in *Rodeo in America* (1996).

There is something about a horse. They are a lot prettier animal than a man is, but not quite as pretty as a woman.

Darrell Arnold
The Cowboy Kind (2001)

And though he later came pretending friendship, the alliance with man would ever be fragile, for the fear he'd struck into their hearts was too deep to be dislodged. Since that neolithic moment when first a horse was haltered, there were those among men who understood this.

NICHOLAS EVANS
The Horse Whisperer (1995)

We have saturated the horse with our emotions. Yet, a lover of horses has nothing to prove and no expertise to reveal. It is important that we find animals to love, and that is the end of the story.

THOMAS MCGUANE
Some Horses (1999)

Most old cowboys can recognize a black and white photo of a horse they rode fifty years ago but can't recognize themselves or their wives.

> RED STEAGALL
> *Ride for the Brand* (1999)

There are friends and faces that may be forgotten, but there are horses that never will be.

> ANDY ADAMS
> *The Log of a Cowboy* (1903)

I loved old Jenny more than anything else in the world.

> JOHN WAYNE (1907–1979), remembering his first horse.

The person that doesn't love a horse has missed a lot of livin'.

R. LEWIS BOWMAN
Bumfuzzled (1992)

Horses and life, it's all the same to me.

BUCK BRANNAMAN (1962–)

No better word can be spoken of a man than that he is careful with his horses.

ANDY ADAMS
The Log of a Cowboy (1903)

Keep plenty of grain in the barn and you'll see that a smart horse never forgets the way home.

OLD COWBOY SAYING

A good horse is worth its feed.

OLD COWBOY SAYING

When in doubt, let your horse figure it out.

OLD COWBOY SAYING

A cattle pony enjoys the work as much as its rider.

THEODORE ROOSEVELT
Hunting Trips of a Ranchman (1885)

A ranch horse is somewhere between a teddy bear and a good pocket knife.

BAXTER BLACK (1945–)

He learned cow.

COWBOY SLANG FOR UNDERSTANDING HOW TO HANDLE CATTLE.

Cow sense

COWBOY PHRASE FOR THE INTELLIGENCE OF THEIR CUTTING HORSES.

Between the shoulder and the hip a horse belongs to the rider; the rest belongs to the ranch.

OLD COWBOY SAYING

It wasn't so hard. You got to where you could sleep on a horse without any trouble.

CHARLES GOODNIGHT, quoted in *Charles Goodnight* (1949).

———

The rough string rider ain't long on brains, but he ain't short on guts, neither.

MACK HUGHES, quoted in *Hashknife Cowboy* (1984).

———

[A cowboy, dismounted, is] just a plain bowlegged human who smelled very horsey at times, slept in his underwear and was subject to boils and dyspepsia.

JO MORA, quoted in *The Cowboys* (1973).

He was not a pretty rider, but a hell of a good rider.

ANONYMOUS COWBOY discussing Theodore Roosevelt, quoted in *An Autobiography* (1913).

Of all the horses I ever rode, I once rode one that was all horse.

OLD COWBOY SAYING

Wild horses was easy to catch compared to gathering horses that was once tame and had gone to the wild bunch.

MACK HUGHES, quoted in *Hashknife Cowboy* (1984).

I'm kind of sorry now so many were caught.... For they really belong, not to man, but to that country of junipers and sage, of deep arroyos, mesas—and freedom.

WILL JAMES (1892–1942)

A horse is considered well-trained when he is convinced that he wants to do what you want him to do.

GLADIOLA MONTANA
Never Ask a Man the Size of his Spread (1993)

A young horse is like a young person; they get tired and bored easy.

TOM DAVIS
Be Tough or Be Gone (1984)

————

When you give a lesson in meanness to a critter or a person, don't act surprised if they learn their lesson.

TEXAS BIX BENDER
Don't Squat With Your Spurs On (1992)

————

The cowboy has no patience for the details of dog training. He didn't take much schooling to be a cowboy, so he figgers the blue heeler shouldn't need much training to be a cowdog.

BAXTER BLACK
Cactus Tracks and Cowboy Philosophy (1997)

A man that says a hoss don't know nothin' don't know much about hosses.

> CHARLES M. RUSSELL
> *Trails Plowed Under* (1927)

Toro could cut the baking powder out of a biscuit without breaking the crust.

> FRANK M. KING, about a cutting horse.
> *Longhorn Trail Drivers* (1940)

Sometimes you just need fast horses.

> Anonymous

When people see a horse running, it fires up their imagination.

MICHAEL MARTIN MURPHEY

———•+•———

That was the toughest ride I ever had.
Nat Love, a.k.a. Deadwood Dick, about riding the wildest horse in the outfit to earn a job.

The Life and Adventures of Nate Love (1907)

———•+•———

To say that somebody is as smart as a cutting horse is to say that he is smarter than a Philadelphia lawyer, smarter than a steel trap, smarter than a coyote, smarter than a Harvard graduate–all combined.

J. FRANK DOBIE
Mustangs and Cow Horses (1941)

Horses and mules could get accustomed to most anything: moose, bears, and strange items they were required to carry, but they drew the line when it came to camels.

> ANDY RUSSELL, on the behavior of horses and mules that encountered the camels some enterprising late-nineteenth-century stockmen and freighters had attempted to use.
> *The Canadian Cowboy*, 1993

Burros have a way of increasin' faster than you can imagine.

> MACK HUGHES, quoted in *Hashknife Cowboy* (1984).

I like ratty stock. I believe as long as a horse or mule are fightin' you, they'll work for you.

TOM DAVIS
Be Tough or Be Gone (1984)

Never walk up behind a mule unless you are tired of the life you are living.

R. LEWIS BOWMAN
Bumfuzzled (1992)

People don't really own mules. They are like cats. They're livin' at your place and doin' as little as they can to get by and still stay there.

BAXTER BLACK
Cactus Tracks and Cowboy Philosophy (1997)

Longhorn cattle? Now, that was something else! She had seen an early photograph of some two dozen steers on her father's ranch . . . and from the first had been fascinated by those incredible horns, jutting out at right angles to the animal's face and reaching for seven feet, with a double twist on the way.

JAMES A. MICHENER
Centennial (1974)

The longhorn bull was one of the nastiest brutes in creation.

ALBERT MARRIN
Cowboys, Indians and Gunfighters (1993)

———

The domestic cattle of Texas, miscalled tame, are fifty times more dangerous to footmen than the fiercest buffalo.

ANONYMOUS

———

A good fence should be pig tight, horse high, and bull strong.

OLD COWBOY SAYING

The cattle industry is, of necessity, a frontier industry.

CLARA M. LOVE
Southwestern Historical Quarterly 1916

———————

These are our cattle. The folks who own the ranch get the money, but we doctor and calve them, and see that they are safe and healthy. . . . So even though we can't take them off anywhere, they belong to the cowboys.

JIM PATTERSON, quoted in *Ride for the Brand* (2000).

———————

You can see all the cows in the world and it won't make a difference until they're your cows.

CORD MCCOY
American Cowboy February 2000

Loyalty to his herd, an ingrained code of fidelity to his trust, kept him rubbing tobacco juice in his eyes to stay awake and risking his life after some wild, crazy brute of a gaunt, ten-dollar cow.

J. FRANK DOBIE
A Vaquero of the Brush Country (1929)

I cannot work a cow unless I am living with them.

ROYCE HANSON
American Cowboy July/August 2000

Blue, you work no more. You'll be the leader of our herd.

CHARLES GOODNIGHT to his legendary ox, Old Blue, who led many a trail drive before dying of old age on Goodnight's ranch, quoted in *Charles Goodnight* (1949).

The only thing dumber than a cow is a black cow. And the only thing dumber than a black cow is somebody that tries to work just one.

CURT BRUMMETT, quoted in Horsing Around (1999).

———•••———

Runnin' a cow outfit is like dancin' with a bear: Yer not done til the bear is.

R. LEWIS BOWMAN
Bumfuzzled (1992)

———•••———

Dealing with range cows . . . is not a job for the squeamish, the vacillating, the short-winded, or the fastidious. One must be able to out-think a thousand pound brute [with] the intellect of a Bartlett pear.

BAXTER BLACK, quoted in *Ranching Traditions* (1989).

Marked her with my teeth—just as good as I could have done it with a knife.

BONE MIZELL, about earmarking a particularly hard-to-handle cow, quoted in *Florida Cow Hunter* (1990).

A young heifer or steer is . . . loath to leave the herd, always tries to break back into it, can run like a deer, and can dodge like a rabbit.

THEODORE ROOSEVELT
Hunting Trips of a Ranchman (1885)

Before the rural cowboy approaches a bound and helpless calf with his diabolical instruments, the cowboy has likely been dragged, butted, bitten, slobbered on, crapped on, and perversely and roundly kicked in several tender areas.

RALPH REYNOLDS
Growing up Cowboy (1991)

If there was one moment that stood out in the mind of the early Texas cowboy, it may have been the memory of putting the first hot iron to the flank of a calf.

DAVE DARY
Cowboy Culture (1989)

———•◦•———

Goodnighting.

Word used to describe the operation performed on bulls where the scrotum was cut off and the testicles sewn into the abdominal cavity. Bulls on cattle drives had a rough go until CHARLES GOODNIGHT developed this procedure, and it did not in any way affect a bull's performance as a breeder, quoted in *Charles Goodnight* (1949).

I'd forgotten, until now, the sheer, blank, bovine stupidity of calves—brains as unsteady as their legs.

BART McDOWELL
The American Cowboy in Life and Legend (1972)

He just stood there like a cow looking at a new gate.

OLD COWBOY SAYING

The only way to drive cattle fast is slowly.

TEXAS BIX BENDER
Don't Squat with your Spurs on (1992)

I was as itchy to [get going] as a cow with her teats in a thistle.

TOM DAVIS
Be Tough or Be Gone (1984)

Lots of smoke, a stampede, but no one killed.

JACK POTTER, discussing a Dodge City six-shooter duel between a cowboy and a gambler, quoted in the *The Long Trail* (1976).

Oddly, when the cattle stampeded they uttered no sound at all. A trail hand sleeping off-watch would suddenly be aware of a deep rumbling, a trembling of the sod beneath him.

WILLIAM H. FORBIS
The Cowboys (1978)

Next to the smell of blood, nothing will stir range cattle like the bellowing of a calf.

ANDY ADAMS
The Log of a Cowboy (1927)

Within one second after an unusual noise, an entire herd of longhorns could be on their feet, dashing in some arbitrary direction, trampling anything that got in its way.

JAMES A. MICHENER
Centennial (1974)

With an indescribable sound of clashing horns and great bodies moving in unison, the herd was up and away like flushed quail. There was no more warning than that first swoosh of sound.

B. M. Bower
"Bad Penny" (1933)

Then it seemed that the herd moved in a great curve, a huge half-moon, with the points and tail almost opposite, a mile apart.

Zane Grey
Riders of the Purple Sage (1912)

Cattle mostly strayed away while "going along" with winter storms, tail to the wind, walking to keep warm.

IKE BLASINGAME
Dakota Cowboy (1964)

———•••———

Yipi ti yi yo, git along little dogies,
It's your misfortune and none of my own.
Yipi ti yi yo, git along little dogies,
You know Wyoming will be your new home.

"Git Along Little Dogies," a traditional drover song

———•••———

Then we rounded 'em up, an' we put 'em in cars, an' that was the end of the Bar-C-Bars.

OLD DROVER SONG

5

I Fought the Law

The Gun that Won the West

SAID OF THE WINCHESTER REPEATING RIFLE.

———•••———

The gun that won the West.

ALSO SAID BY MANY COWBOYS AND OTHERS OF THE COLT
SIX-SHOOTER OR REVOLVER.

God made some men big and some men small, but Sam Colt evened things up.

<small>COLTS' SLOGAN RESPONSIBLE FOR THE SIX-SHOOTER BEING DUBBED "THE EQUALIZER."</small>

Nobody used anything but a Colt.

<small>"PUT" PUTNEY, Texas Ranger quoted in
Guns and the Gunfighters (1975).</small>

No . . . [cowboy] with any sense ever carried more than five cartridges in a six-shooter, because if he dropped the gun it had the nasty habit of falling on its hammer, which generally . . . allowed it to fire.

<small>ANDY RUSSELL
The Canadian Cowboy (1993)</small>

Most cowboys think it's an infringement on their rights to give up shooting in town.

> MR. McNULTA, quoted in *The Log of a Cowboy* (1903).

Your strap on your chaps, your spurs and your gun—
You're goin' to town to have a little fun.

> OLD COWBOY SONG

Sure glad to see you, but hand me those guns.

> WILD BILL HICKOK, greeting cowboys new to Abilene, Kansas, where Hickok was marshal in 1871, quoted in *Guns and the Gunfighters* (1975).

We protest against so much arming by our police. It may be well enough for our marshal and his assistants to go armed, but one six-shooter is enough. It is too much to see double armed men walking our peaceful streets. . . . Don't let us by too big a show of derringers, lead strangers to imagine that order is only to be maintained by the use of them. One pistol is enough and that should be concealed as much as possible.

ELLSWORTH REPORTER 14 August 1973

In some parts of the land the law is a grown-up force, but it's not grown up out here. It's simply a child. And one poor sheriff has less chance of keeping order among these wild men . . .

MAX BRAND
"The Werewolf" (1926)

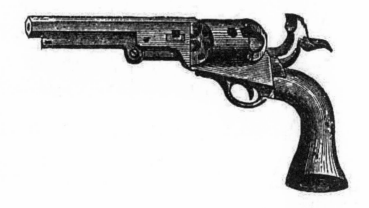

Hickok carried the same equipment he always carried to keep the peace in Abilene: two .44 Colts strapped to his hips, a Bowie knife visible under his Prince Albert, a sawed-off shotgun in the crook of his elbow—plus, no doubt, the pair of .41 Derringers he usually concealed somewhere on his person. He was a terrible walking arsenal.

JOHN JAKES
The Lawless (1978)

Never allow a man to get the drop on you.

WILD BILL HICKOK (1837–1876)

———◦•••◦———

[Happy Jack Jackson] had a penchant for going on periodic drunks of enormous proportions and was adept at scaring the hell out of everybody by shooting flies indoors with his Colt .45 . . .

ANDY RUSSELL
The Canadian Cowboy (1993)

———◦•••◦———

When we hit town it was our intention and ambition to paint the town red. Two months on the dusty plains made us thirsty and wild.

NAT LOVE
The Life and Adventures of Nat Love (1907)

If someone outdraws you, smile and walk away.
You can look tough later, when you're out of sight.

OLD COWBOY SAYING

Though [Hickok's] life was bloody and adventurous, yet he was the champion of the weak and
oppressed; and if he was not a paragon of excel-
lence, he was at least a man of brave impulses.

The Yankton Press and Dakotaian 1 March 1877

It took a fight to bring out the fighter in him, and a
fighter was what he mostly was.

LARRY MCMURTRY
Lonesome Dove (1985)

Perhaps I may yet die with my boots on.

> WILD BILL HICKOK (1837–1876), who did die with his boots on.

———

A cowboy might take cold if he's not wearing his six-shooter.

> Anonymous

———

He was the most skilled gambler, and the nerviest, fastest, deadliest man with a six-gun I ever saw.

> WYATT EARP (1848–1929), referring to Doc Holliday.

He died of lead poisoning.

> Old cowboy saying for a man who'd been shot.

———•••———

They are a tough bunch. They all pack guns.

> ZANE GREY, quoted in *Zane Grey, Romancing the West* (1997).

———•••———

Out West, you lived a long time. Even horse thieves had to hang five minutes longer than anywhere else.

> Anonymous

After killing Billy the Kid if Pat Garrett needed a
friend he would have to buy a dog.

BILL KELLY
"Famous Law Dogs of the Old West: Pat Garrett"
American Western Magazine May 2002

Trouble followed Hopalong Cassidy like wolves follow a snow-driven herd, but few men were more fitted to cope with it than the silver-haired gunfighter.

LOUIS L'AMOUR
The Rustlers of West Fork (1951)

No man in the wrong can stand up to a man in the right who just keeps on a-comin'.

TEXAS RANGER CREED

All a man needed to start a brand of his own was a rope, a runnin' iron, and the nerve to use it.

Old cowboy saying

His calves don't suck the right cows.

What cowboys said about a rustler.
RAMON ADAMS
Cowboy Lingo (1936)

Many a cowboy got his start [by rustling] and got to be a respected cattleman. They was to be respected for they took many chances.

WILL JAMES
The American Cowboy (1942)

It was easy for these characters to stay lost in cattle country because, among cowboys, close inquiry about a man's past was considered discourteous.

WILLIAM H. FORBIS
The Cowboys (1978)

Yet, after all, why should not these equal outcasts of civilization cling together?

BRET HARTE
"Three Vagabonds of Trinidad" (1900)

Well, my dear, you won't have to darn them any-
more.

> BRONCO SAM STEWART, as he shot his wife for mocking
> the way Sam looked in the clothes she darned for him,
> quoted in *Sinners & Saints* (1994).

———•••———

Dear Colonel: . . . I have shot a lady in the eye. But,
Colonel, I was not shooting at the lady. I was
shooting at my wife.

> A cowboy known only as "Gitto" explaining his plight
> in a letter to Theodore Roosevelt, quoted in
> *An Autobiography* (1913).

Deer sur

we have brand 800 caves this roundup we have made sum hay potatoes is a fare crop. That Inglishman yu lef in charge . . . got to fresh and we had to kill the son of a bitch. Nothing much has hapened sence yu lef.

Yurs truely, Jim

LETTER FROM A COWBOY TO AN ABSENTEE RANCH OWNER, quoted in *The Trail Drivers of Texas* (1925).

———

Pistols are almost as numerous as men. It is no longer thought to be an affair of any importance to take the life of a fellow being.

NATHAN A. BAKER
Cheyenne Leader 13 October 1868

Killing men is my specialty. I look at it as a business proposition, and I think I have a corner on the market.

TOM HORN, quoted in *Tom Horn* (1991).

———

The more ignorant you are, the quicker you fight.

WILL ROGERS (1879–1935)

———

I never saw so much useless killing.

BOB KENNON, discussing El Paso, Texas, in the early 1900s.
From the Pecos to the Powder (1965)

When [Sim Roberts] died in Butte in the late twenties I remember that his passing was the occasion for several glorious benders, both in relief and celebration.

> SPIKE VAN CLEVE, writing about a cowhand who "had a propensity for shooting people."
> *Forty Years' Gatherin's* (1977)

The gentleman who has "killed his man" is by no means a *rara avis*. . . . This ubiquitous individual may be seen almost anywhere.

Kansas City Journal 15 November 1881

—◦•••◦—

We beat the drum lowly and shook the spurs slowly
And bitterly west we bore him along;
For we all loved our comrade, so brave and so handsome,
We loved our comrade, although he'd done wrong.

"Streets of Laredo," c. 1860

Roy Bean, out of a combination of boredom, greed, and vanity, had recently appointed himself judge of a vast jurisdiction—the trans-Pecos West—and nowadays hung people freely, often over differences amounting to no more than fifty cents.

JOHN JAKES
The Lawless (1978)

Judge, I was a-talkin' then, but I'm a-swearin' now.

BONE MIZELL, rebutting while on the stand what he'd previously said to be fact, quoted in *Florida Cow Hunter* (1990).

Most train robbers ain't smart, which is a lucky thing for the railroads. . . . Five smart train robbers could bust every railroad in the country.

> LARRY MCMURTRY
> *Streets of Laredo* (1993)

Rustlers are a lazy set when they're not on a ride.

> ZANE GREY
> *Riders of the Purple Sage* (1912)

I never stole a horse in my life—leastways from a white man. I don't count Indians nor the Government, of course.

> JAP HUNT, quoted in *Theodore Roosevelt: An Autobiography* (1913)

What do you want to go and get me arrested for? I have stole thousands of cattle and put your mark and brand on them, and just because I have stole a couple of hundred from you, you go and have me indicted.

> BONE MIZELL, to a crooked judge who was indicting him for stealing some of the judge's cattle, quoted in *Florida Cow Hunter* (1990).

We [Texas Rangers] always rode in two's. If a man made a move, we always tried to see who could hit him first.

> "PUT" PUTNEY, Texas Ranger, quoted in *Guns and the Gunfighters* (1975).

It is to be feared that a great part of [the West] will form a lawless interval between the abodes of civilized men.

WASHINGTON IRVING (1783–1859)

There were scores of shipping points in Kansas for Texas cattle. Of these, only four or five have gained a national reputation as wild and wooly towns.

FLOYD B. STREETER
Prairie Trails and Cow Towns (1936)

Dodge City is one town where the average bad man of the West not only finds his equal, but finds himself badly handicapped.

ANDY ADAMS
The Log of a Cowboy (1903)

Beautiful, bibulous Babylon of the trail.

ANONYMOUS COWBOY DESCRIBING DODGE CITY

Kansas sheep dip

TEXAS DROVER SLANG FOR WHISKEY

In Nevada, for a time, the lawyer, the editor, the banker, the chief desperado, the chief gambler, and the saloon-keeper, occupied the same level in society, and it was the highest. The cheapest and easiest way to become an influential man and be looked up to by the community at large, was to stand behind a bar, wear a cluster-diamond pin, and sell whisky.

MARK TWAIN
Roughing It (1872)

They've got booze [in that town] that would make
a pet rabbit fight a wolf.

ANONYMOUS HORSE TRADER, quoted in *The Log of a
Cowboy* (1903).

Never hire the people you drink with.

OLD COWBOY SAYING

[Cowboys] are far from being as lawless as they are described; though they sometimes cut queer antics when, after many months of lonely life, they come into a frontier town in which drinking and gambling are the only recognized forms of amusement, and where pleasure and vice are considered synonymous terms.

THEODORE ROOSEVELT
Hunting Trips of a Ranchman (1885)

Unhappily, the drunken bully and gambler of America and Mexico has found the six-shooter convenient, and carries it more regularly than his tooth-pick.

London Daily Telegraph 22 October 1869

Hell, any place in Montana's a good place for a saloon.

> HUB HICKOX, quoted in Forty Years' Gatherin's (1977).

Good whiskey and bad women will be the ruin of you varmints.

> BARNEY MCCANN, to the other drovers, quoted in *The Log of a Cowboy* (1903).

From girls in their teens, launching out on a life of shame, to the adventuress who had once had youth and beauty in her favor, but was now discarded and ready for the final dose of opium and the coroner's verdict,—all were there in tinsel and paint.

> ANDY ADAMS, referring to Dodge City in the 1880s. *The Log of a Cowboy* (1903)

Soiled doves, *nymphs du prairie*, calico queens, painted cats

DROVER SLANG FOR PROSTITUTES.

The Devil's Addition

DROVER SLANG FOR ABILENE'S RED LIGHT DISTRICT.

Whatever a trail-weary man wanted, from new red-top boots with stars and crescent moons cut into leather, to groceries to a bath to a woman—he could find it in Abilene.

JOHN JAKES
The Lawless (1978)

There is a mania for gambling in Newton. The heart of every man who has been here long enough to dig down a little to the substrata of life, nestles the germ of this passion. In some it has bloomed into a full blown flower.

Topeka Daily Commonwealth 17 September 1871

He had discovered years ago that the good opinion of a rube was a free ticket to the bigger games in a strange town.

MARILYN DURHAM
Dutch Uncle (1973)

Poker is a science; the highest court in Texas has said so.

QUINCE FORREST, quoted in *The Log of a Cowboy* (1903).

When you call me that, smile!

THE VIRGINIAN, in response to a threat from Trampas. Archetype for all fictional western confrontations from that point onward.
OWEN WISTER
The Virginian (1902)

Hey, you damn sonofabitch cowboy. Go get a gun and get to work.

> DOC HOLLIDAY (1851–1887), to Ike Clanton, the day before the infamous Gunfight at the O.K. Corral.

Don't shoot me. I don't want to fight.

> BILLY CLANTON (1862–1881), just before the Gunfight at the O.K. Corral.

That fight didn't take but about 30 seconds, and it seems like, in my going on 80 years, we could find some other happenings to discuss.

> WYATT EARP (1848–1929), about the Gunfight at the O.K. Corral.

Good-bye, Emmet. Don't surrender: die game.

> BOB DALTON'S (1869–1892) words to his brother as he lay dying in Death Alley after an aborted robbery attempt of the Condon Bank in Coffeyville, Kansas, quoted in Joseph G. Rosa, *Age of the Gunfighter* (1993).

Many a cowboy out on the lonely plains has been buried with a clean bandana spread over his face to keep the dirt . . . from touching it.

> JOHN YOUNG, quoted in *A Vaquero of the Brush Country* (1929).

Take me to Boot Hill and cover me with roses, I'm just a young cowboy and I know I done wrong.

> OLD COWBOY SONG

6

And They Call the Thing Rodeo

Rodeoing is an existential thing. You're on your own. Ultimately it is the human condition. Whether you succeed or fail depends on your mental attitude.

KEN "BUTCH" COX
American Cowboy September/October 2000

———◆◆◆◆◆———

Being wild, being free, being crazy is critical to rodeo.

BERNIE SMYTH, quoted in *Rodeo in America* (1996).

There are no gimmies in rodeo.

TY MURRAY
Roughstock (2001)

———•••••———

I need to thank my mom for loaning me the money to rodeo this year.

MICKEY GEE
American Cowboy March/April 2000

———•••••———

A guy can be a world champion and still have to live with his parents.

GAVIN EHRINGER
Western Horseman

So many things can go wrong before anything goes right.

DEE PICKETT
American Cowboy July/August 1999

———

I just came here to ride good and make some money.

LAN LA JEUNESS
American Cowboy March/April 2000

———

In the old times, . . . a rodeo was a formal and stately affair. It was held in turns upon the estates of the owners. . . . Such a gathering commonly included from twelve to twenty proprietors, each attended by from six to fifteen vaqueros, and with six or eight horses.

CHARLES NORDHOFF, quoted in *The Best of the West* (1991).

There never was a horse that couldn't be rode,
There never was a rider that couldn't be throwed.

OLD COWBOY SAYING

The first thing I do after I get on [a green horse for the first time] is get the hell off.

CRAIG CAMERON
American Cowboy January/February 2001

He didn't buck me off, but he used me plumb up.

BUCK BRANNAMAN
The Faraway Horses (2001)

Riding a bronc is like dancing with a girl: You just fall into the rhythm. But you've got to know your business. If not, you'll either pop your gizzard or eat dirt.

CASEY TIBBS (1929–1980)

—•••—

Worst Outlaw in the World—The Horse Which Threw the Best of Them.

POSTER FROM IRWIN BROTHERS WILD WEST SHOW, Cheyenne Frontier Days, perhaps the only such enterprise to feature a horse as the star, quoted in *Steamboat, Legendary Bucking Horse* (1992).

I had my head snapped back until I thought it was going to come off, and I felt as if my lungs were going to burst . . .

CLAYTON DANKS, on riding Steamboat, quoted in *Steamboat, Legendary Bucking Horse* (1992).

[A bucking bronco] warped his backbone and hallelujahed all over the lot.

RAMON F. ADAMS (1889–1976)

[That bronc will] stamp you in the ground so deep you'll take root and disappear.

OLD COWBOY SAYING

A beast with a bellyfull of bed springs.

COWBOY SAYING FOR A BUCKING HORSE

———◦•◦•◦———

There's about a quarter of an inch between hero and idiot.

SPEED WILLIAMS, about rodeo riders.
American Cowboy March/April 2000

———◦•◦•◦———

The guy who tries hardest wins.

TY MURRAY
Roughstock (2001)

I'd rather hit the dirt than just get by. If I lose, better to go down trying.

BILLY ETBAUER
American Cowboy March/April 2000

I credit my success to the fact that I was never content or satisfied.

FRED WHITFIELD (1967–)

If it weren't for my damned old black face I'd have been boss of one of these divisions long ago.

JIM PERRY, top hand, commenting on his lot with the famed XIT Ranch during the nineteenth century, quoted in *The Real American Cowboy* (1985).

And no doubt he would have.

Anonymous white cowboy who worked with JIM PERRY at the XIT, quoted in *The Real American Cowboy* (1985).

Just keep riding bulls like you do—and turn white.

FRECKLES BROWN, answering black bull rider Myrtis Dightman's question, "How can I win the world?" Brown was acknowledging the truth of the judging years ago that was tainted by racism, quoted in *Gold Buckle*, 1995.

As far as rodeo fans are concerned, I don't think skin color has anything to do with it.

FRED WHITFIELD (1967–), first black PRCA World Champion All-Around Cowboy

Horses get all the credit for my rodeo days.

> LARRY MAHAN (1943–), six-time World Champion All-Around Cowboy.

Gold medals are something special. They aren't just another saddle hanging in the corner.

> JOE BEAVER
> *American Cowboy* July/August 2001

It's not like my life won't be complete if I don't win. I try as hard as I can every single ride. That's the best I can do. That's the best anyone can do.

> TY MURRAY (1969–)

Ty's the greatest cowboy I've ever seen.

> TUFF HEDEMAN (1963–), speaking of his friend, Ty
> Murray.

The story of Lane Frost is a simple one. He'd help in the chutes, never said no to a fan, never kicked at the earth or threw his hat in public after an unfair low score. A good friend, a good husband.

> KELLIE FROST
> Cheyenne, 1993 Statue Dedication

He left everybody with a smile.

> TUFF HEDEMAN (1963–), in a tribute to Lane Frost.

Loves to buck cowboys off.

> TED NUCE, World Champion Bull Rider 1983, about Red Rock, the 1987 Championship Riding Bull.

Horses are smarter, but bulls are more curious.

> JOHN GROWNEY, quoted in *Gold Buckle* (1995).

The thing I don't like about this bull riding, is that you have to get on that damned bull.

> MYRTIS DIGHTMAN, quoted in *Gold Buckle* (1995).

And yes, those front teeth are fake. They fill in for the pair punched out by a bull's horn before he was old enough to shave.

> KENDRA SANTOS
> *Ring of Fire* (2000)

Folks that have never ridden bulls or broncs or clowned usually don't know how it feels for that eight seconds. Sometimes, everything is a blur. Sometimes, everything is extremely clear, but it feels like you're getting every third frame in a movie.

GEORGE WILHITE
"Red Malone"
American Western Magazine February 2002

The bulls will let me know when it's time to retire.

STEVE TOMAC, bullfighter, quoted in *Rodeo in America* (1996).

I'm not a clown. I'm sorry, but I'm not out there . . . to be funny. There's too much at stake.

RONNY SPARKS, about his bullfighting to protect rodeo's bull riders, quoted in *Rodeo in America*, 1996.

[Rodeo-clowning] was like Vietnam. You had to accomplish a mission and protect your friends.

KEN "BUTCH" COX, ex-bullfighter
American Cowboy September/October 2000

If yer in the corral and one of yer friends gets bucked off, everybody runs over there . . . to make sure he's all right. If he's alive, ya start tellin' the story right away. If he's dead, you wait a couple of days.

BAXTER BLACK
Cactus Tracks and Cowboy Philosophy (1997)

There's not a whiff of pampered athlete syndrome within a thousand miles of here.

KENDRA SANTOS
Ring of Fire (2000)

It's bull riders who put themselves daily in peril.

They crack skulls, break bones, and spill out their
marrow.

But them boys, ever' one, 'fore they climb on their
bull,

When tightenin' their bull ropes, before they yell,
"Pull!"

Their hearts are as meek as an innocent child's.

Their minds and their souls are both humble and
mild.

They ride, but they're thinking, "God, yer will be
done.

That's why I ride with 'em with each risin' sun."

FROM "THE BULL RIDER'S PRAYER"
K. T. Etling

7

End of the Trail

The West is dead! You may lose a sweetheart, but you won't forget her.

> CHARLES M. RUSSELL, quoted in *Charlie Russell Journal* (1997)

———•⋅•⋅•———

The cowboy will never die.

> WILL JAMES
> *The American Cowboy* (1942)

———•⋅•⋅•———

In a narrow grave just six by three,
They laid him there on the lone prairie.

> ANONYMOUS, from "O Bury Me Not on the Lone
> Prairie," old cowboy song, c. late 19th century

———◦•◦———

Old Steamboat, the grand old horse of the passing west, is dead. The horse that has nipped in the bud the fondest hopes of many a broncho buster, the horse that has sent fear into the ranks of the veteran busters is no more.

> *Cheyenne Daily Leader* 15 October 1914

Saint Peter, open up that ... gate, for ... a real cowboy [is] coming ... riding old Steamboat bareback.

> WILL ROGERS, at Charlie Irwin's death, quoted in *Steamboat, Legendary Bucking Horse* (1992).

They say there will be a great round-up
And cowboys, like dogies, will stand,
to be marked by the Riders of Judgment
Who are posted and know every brand.

> OLD COWBOY SONG

When I die you can skin me and put me on top of Trigger, and I'll be happy.

> ROY ROGERS (1911–1998)

Hellfire, no, you ain't going to wash him. You all know he'd never allow it if he was alive and you all ain't going to take advantage of him now he's dead.

> BONE MIZELL, after the death of his good friend, John Underhill, quoted in *Florida Cow Hunter* (1990)

Tom Blasingame lived [alone] at the Campbell Creek camp for over fifty years. He went out . . . to check his cows, and his horse came back . . . trailing his reins. They found him on the prairie, hands folded over his chest. He just laid down and went to sleep. He was ninety-one.

> RED STEAGALL
> *Ride for the Brand* (2000)

He was the best cowman, the most practical Westerner, that I ever saw.

> ANDY ADAMS, about CHARLES GOODNIGHT, quoted in
> *Charles Goodnight* (1949).

The cowboy was the last of [his] kind, and he's mighty near extinct.

> CHARLES M. RUSSELL
> *Trails Plowed Under* (1927)

It seems now as though it was all in some other world, and under fairer skies.

> JOHN G. JACOBS, quoted in *The Long Trail* (1976)

In that land we led a free and hardy life, with horse and with rifle.

THEODORE ROOSEVELT
Theodore Roosevelt: An Autobiography (1913)

Three things swept [the cowboy] away—the exhausting of the virgin pastures, the coming of the wire fence, and Mr. Armour of Chicago, who set the price to suit himself.

OWEN WISTER, quoted in *Frederic Remington* (1999).

Only a few of us are left now ... scattered from Texas to Canada. The rest have left the wagon and gone ahead across the big divide, looking for a new range. I hope they find good water and plenty of grass. ... Wherever they are is where I want to go.

E. C. "TEDDY BLUE" ABBOTT
We Pointed Them North (1939)

Cow folks are scarce now ... but thiy left tracks in history that the farmer cant plow under.

CHARLES M. RUSSELL in a letter to George W. Farr, 12 March 1919.
Charlie Russell Journal (1997)

And what has become of [the cowboys]? . . . Except where he lingers in the mountains of New Mexico he has been dispersed.

OWEN WISTER
The Virginian (1902)

I have always regretted that I didn't live about thirty or forty years earlier, and in the same old country—the Indian Territory. I would have liked to have gotten there ahead of . . . the barbed wire fence.

WILL ROGERS (1879–1935)

The broad and boundless prairies have already been bounded and will soon be made narrow.

THEODORE ROOSEVELT
Hunting Trips of a Ranchman (1885)

A whole lot of sorry things can happen to a fence.

ANONYMOUS COWBOY, quoted in *The Cowboys* (1973).

A man wearing clean dry clothes and sitting in a pickup can't understand our plight.

JOHN R. ERICKSON
LZ Cowboy (1996)

The cowboy is slowly riding into the sunset because of economic conditions we no longer control—because every year there are fewer ranches and fewer cowboys.

BOBBY NEWTON
American Cowboy September/October 2000

We used to make boots to fit a stirrup. Now we make them to fit the gas pedal of a Cadillac.

> Cosimo Lucchese, whose family has been bootmakers to the cowboys since 1883.

People on horses look better than they are, people in cars look worse.

> MARYA MANNES (1904–1990)

Mike didn't like cars anyway, and on the old road he could forget about them, and feel more like himself.

> WALTER VAN TILBURG CLARK
> "The Wind and the Snow of Winter" (1944)

Cowboys don't have as soft a time as they did eight or ten years ago. I remember when we set around the fire the winter through and didn't do a lick of work for five or six months of the year, except to chop a little wood to build a fire.

ANONYMOUS COWBOY, c. 1900, quoted in *Trail Driving Days* (1925).

We were cowboys, pretty good ones, and we wouldn't have traded places with anyone in the world.

JOHN R. ERICKSON
LZ Cowboy (1996)

See that son? That's God's own handiwork. Look around you. This is my church.

> REX ALLEN talking to his son while outside his Sonoita, Arizona, ranch.
> *American Cowboy* March/April 2000

The great free ranches . . . must pass away . . . and we who have felt the charm of the life . . . must also feel real sorrow that those who come after us are not to see . . . the . . . most exciting phase of American existence.

> THEODORE ROOSEVELT
> *Ranch Life and the Hunting Trail* (1888)

You can run more dudes to the acre than you can cattle.

> ANONYMOUS, quoted in *The Real American Cowboy* (1985).

———•••———

We used to run an outfit,
The greatest in the West;
Our cowboys were the wonders—
Our roundups were the best;
The punchers still are with us,
But now they merely guide
The tenderfoot from Boston
Who's learnin' how to ride.

> ARTHUR CHAPMAN
> "The Dude Ranch"
> *Out Where the West Begins* (1917)

VACATIONS
FOR SALE
CHEAP!

in the

WEST

In 1883, William F. Cody discovered there was more money in show business than in hunting and scouting.

ALBERT MARRIN
Cowboys, Indians and Gunfighters (1993)

A company of Wild West cowboys. The real rough riders of the world whose daring exploits have made their very names synonymous with deeds of bravery.

POSTER FOR BUFFALO BILL'S WILD WEST SHOW

History and romance died when the plow turned the country grass side down.

CHARLES RUSSELL, quoted in *From the Pecos to the Powder* (1965).

All my interests are still with the west—the modern west.

BUFFALO BILL CODY (1846–1917)

When you're really down and out, you look at your hole card, and our western way of life is reminiscent of the way things used to be.

KEN OVERCAST
American Cowboy November/December 2001

The feel for the cowboy is everywhere; the symbol of the cowboy is just as pervasive.

JOE B. FRANTZ
The Frontier Re-examined (1967)

The golden age of the real cowboy in the American West was gone as the twentieth century dawned. Yet cowboy culture was still glowing brightly in the minds of Americans.

DAVE DARY
Cowboy Culture (1989)

There is no way you can compare the cowboy's lifestyle to any other, no matter how hard you try.

CURT BRUMMETT, quoted in *Horsing Around* (1999).

I try to take people away from the immediate moment to another place, another time.

WADDIE MITCHELL

I know of none of the boys still living, for in the years that have passed we have become separated like the trail dust we made.

BOB KENNON
From the Pecos to the Powder (1965)

Many Montanans see their homeland turning . . . into a virtual theme park full of designer-dressed Westerners who don't understand what it really takes to make a living on the land.

DAVID MCCUMBER
The Cowboy Way (1999)

Somewhere up ahead were towns where he had never been, country he had never seen. The trail stretched out before him, a line of possibilities worn in the sand.

LOUIS L'AMOUR
The Trail to Seven Pines (1951)

————

Maybe the American cowboy represents the last of the free men.

CASEY TIBBS (1929–1990)

————

Until we meet again, may the good Lord take a liking to you.

ROY ROGERS (1911–1998)

Those who still cowboy, do it because they love it and do so with the hope that they are keeping alive a way of life that few others could withstand and absolutely cannot understand.

CURT BRUMMETT, quoted in *Horsing Around* (1999).

The legacy of the American cowboy will only get stronger as the world changes.

DANN DUFFY
American Cowboy February 2000

The Old West is not a certain place in a certain time, it's a state of mind. It's whatever you want it to be.

TOM MIX (1880–1940)

Who's Who

Abbott, E. C., also known as " 'Teddy Blue," was a drover and cowpuncher during the days of the great trail herds. Blue's recollections were written down in *We Pointed Them North: Recollections of a Cowpuncher*.

Adams, Andy, was a drover and cowpuncher who trailed herds north in the late 1800s.

Adams, Ramon, was a cowboy historian.

Allen, Guy "The Legend," is a sixteen-time world steer roping PRCA champion from Vinita, Oklahoma.

Allen, James, is a nine-time National Finals Rodeo steer roping qualifier and father of Guy Allen.

Allen, Rex, was a popular TV and movie cowboy from Sonoita, Arizona.

Arnold, Darrell, is a working cowboy and writer.

Autry, Gene, was a telegrapher for the railroad before he became the best known of Hollywood's singing cowboys. Autry starred in movies, a TV series, and was a recording artist.

Bean, Roy, was a legendary American frontier judge.

Beasley, Parry, has cowboyed all over Wyoming. He is currently employed at Cody's Valley Ranch.

Beaver, Joe, is a three-time PRCA World Champion All-Around Cowboy and five-time PRCA World Champion Calf-Roper.

Bender, Texas Bix, is a cowboy humorist, and former writer for the television show *Hee Haw*.

Billy the Kid, famed outlaw of the West, his real name was probably Henry McCarty, but he is usually referenced as William H. Bonney. He was shot by Sheriff Pat F. Garrett.

Black, Baxter, is a veterinarian-turned-cowboy poet, NPR commentator, and columnist who has written twelve books.

Blasingame, Ike, was a Matador cowboy during that ranch's heyday near the beginning of the twentieth century. He cowboyed for the Matador in both Texas and on lands leased from the Cheyenne Indian Nation.

Bower, B. M. (Bertha Muzzy), was a popular western fiction writer.

Bowman, R. Lewis, is an Arizona cowboy, cattleman, author, and chronicler of the cowboy way of life. Lewis has done the Western world a service by cataloguing cowboy sayings, witticisms, and colloquialisms he's heard or remembered through the years.

Boxleitner, Bruce, is a Hollywood cowboy, actor, and has co-hosted the Los Angeles Pro/Celebrity Rodeo.

Branch, Edward Douglas, was a western historian and writer.

Brand, Max, was one of the pen name of Frederick Faust. He created Dr. Kildare, Destry, and many other popular fictional characters.

Brannaman, Buck, is a horse gentler, who has started more than 10,000 young horses in his clinics over the past eighteen years. He served as advisor on the set of Robert Redford's movie of *The Horse Whisperer* (the main character in the bestseller and movie was based largely on him).

Brown, Freckles, was a bull rider who died in 1987, and Lane Frost's mentor.

Brown, J. P. S., author of *The Outfit*, which was the first contemporary novel placed in the Cowboy Hall of Fame library

Brummett, Curt, has been a cowboy, rancher, oil field worker, and popular western humorist with tall tales to tell from all his west Texas and New Mexico experiences.

Burrows, G. D., an old time trail driver who resided in Del Rio, Texas, toward the end of his life.

Calamity Jane, born Martha Canary, was known for drinking hard, wearing men's clothes, chewing tobacco, and shooting well. She was a Pony Express rider and scout before performing in Buffalo Bill's Wild West Show.

Cameron, Craig, is a Texas cowboy, rancher, ex-bull rider, and noted horse trainer.

Cather, Willa, American short-story writer and novelist.

Chapman, Arthur, was a cowboy poet.

Christian, Jim, was a working cowboy.

Clanton, Billy, youngest member of the notorious Clanton Gang, he was killed by Wyatt Earp during the infamous gunfight at the O.K. Corral in Tombstone, Arizona.

Clark, Walter Van Tilburg, was a popular western novelist, most famous for *The Ox-Bow Incident*.

Clay, John Randolph, was a writer of the Old West.

Cody, Buffalo Bill, was born William Frederick Cody in Iowa in 1846. Before founding his Wild West Show, he had been a trapper, a bullwhacker, a Colorado "Fifty-Niner," Pony Express rider, wagonmaster, stagecoach driver, Civil War soldier, hotel manager, and prairie scout of the Indian Wars.

Coleman, Evans, was an old time Arizona cowpuncher.

Cox, Ken "Butch," is a well-known rodeo clown.

Cunninghame Graham, R. B., was a Scottish writer who lived as a cattle rancher in Argentina.

Dalton, Bob, was a deputy marshal for the federal court in Wichita, Kansas, before joining his brothers in the notorious Doolin-Dalton Gang.

Danks, Clayton, was born in 1879 in Nebraska. He worked at Wyoming's Bosler Ranch as a cowboy and began rodeoing in 1903. He rode Steamboat to his second World Championship at the 1909 Cheyenne Frontier Days.

Dary, David, is an American chronicler of the West and professor at the University of Kansas.

Davis, Tom, is a cowboy who in 1976 rode his horse and led a pack train from El Paso, Texas, to Fairbanks, Alaska. The 4,500-mile journey took Davis six months to complete.

Day, H. C., was the father of Harry and grandfather of Sandra Day O'Connor; H. C. went partners on the Lazy B and ended up owning and running the entire ranch.

Day, Harry "DA," (pronounced "Dee-ay"), was the father of Supreme Court Justice Sandra Day O'Connor. DA and his wife, Ada Mae or "MO" (pronounced "Em-oh"), lived their entire married lives at the Lazy B, a 160,000-acre ranch that straddled the boundary between Arizona and New Mexico.

Dightman, Myrtis, was the first black cowboy to qualify for the National Finals back in 1964 and also Charles Sampson's mentor.

Dobie, J. Frank, was a cowman before he became a folklorist, a professor, and a writer during the early part of the twentieth century.

Duffy, Dann, is an Arizona cowboy who today makes his living helping tourists live the Western experience.

Durham, Marilyn, is the wry Indiana-born novelist who wrote the bestseller *The Man Who Loved Cat Dancing*.

Earp, Wyatt, was a law officer, gambler, and gunfighter, and served as marshal in Wichita and Dodge City. He later became an armed guard for the Wells, Fargo Company in Tombstone, Arizona, where, with his brothers Virgil and Morgan and a friend, Doc Holliday, he was involved in the controversial gunfight at the O.K. Corral.

Eastwood, Clint, has played numerous film and TV cowboys, including Rowdy Yates in *Rawhide* and the Man With No Name in Franco Zefferelli's popular spaghetti western—*A Fistful of Dollars*. He was awarded two Oscars—Best Picture and Best Director—for his film *Unforgiven* in which he starred as William Munny.

Ehringer, Gavin, rodeo cowboy (Western Horseman) and co-author of *Rodeo in America*.

Elliott, Sam, is the roughhewn actor best known for playing laconic cowboys.

Erickson, John R., is a former working cowboy, and now a writer and creator of "Hank the Cowdog."

Estelman, Loren D., is a writer of both mysteries and historical westerns.

Etbauer, Billy, is a PRCA World Champion Saddle Bronc Rider from Ree Heights, South Dakota.

Etling, K. T. (Kathy), the editor of this book, is an enthusiast for all things Western and has cowboyed on several ranches in Wyoming. She is a charter member of the Missouri Cowboy Poets Association.

Evans, Clay Bonnyman, worked on ranches from Laramie, Wyoming, to Cimarron, New Mexico, and California's San Joaquin Valley. He is now a columnist and book editor for the *Boulder Daily Camera*.

Evans, Dale, was born Frances Octavia Smith in Uvalde, Texas. Smith grew up to marry Leonard Slye, the birth name of cowboy star Roy Rogers. Dale was known as the "Queen of the West" and starred along with Roy in the *Roy Rogers* TV series, as well as western movies.

Evans, Nicholas, is a London-based, best-selling author of *The Horse Whisperer*, source of a major motion picture with Robert Redford.

Flood, Jim, was a trail boss during the late 1800s for Texas cattleman Don Lovell.

Forbis, William H., was born in cowboy country in Montana, and worked as an editor for *Time*, covering art, theater, and cinema.

Ford, John, was a noted director of many legendary western movies.

Forrest, Quince, was a cowboy in the late 1800s.

Frantz, Joe B, has written extensively on the American frontier.

Frost, Lane, was a PRCA champion bull rider who died after being gored by a bull at Cheyenne Frontier Days. The movie *8 Seconds* depicts Frost's life in rodeo.

Garrett, Pat, was the sheriff who shot Billy the Kid.

Gee, Mickey, is a World Champion Steer Wrestler.

Gibson, Hoot, was both a popular cowboy movie star and side-kick during the height of the western movie's popularity.

Goodnight, Charles, was a Texas Ranger who went on to become one of the most successful cowmen in Texas.

Grey, Zane, was a hugely successful and influential writer of melodramatic tales of the Old West.

Growney, John, is a former bull rider who is now a successful rodeo stock contractor from Red Bluff, California.

Hanson, Royce, cowboys in South Dakota. Hanson rode the range when life was still quite primitive by modern standards.

Hargo, Dwayne, has competed in the Wrangler Bullfight Tour since 1986 and has won the world title.

Harte, Bret, was the editor of *The Overland Monthly* and is famous for his many stories of the West.

Hedeman, Richard "Tuff," is a champion bull rider who helped co-found the Professional Bull Riders' Association (PBR).

Hickok, Wild Bill (James Butler), was the flamboyant and feared lawman who was marshal of Hays City, Kansas (where he enforced a no-guns policy), and later Abilene. In 1876, he was shot in the back of the head in a Deadwood, South Dakota, saloon.

Hickox, Hub, founded the town of Melville, Montana, in 1879 or 1880.

Higley, Brewster, is reputed to have written the classic"Home on the Range."

Holliday, Doc (John Henry), was the notorious dentist-turned-gunfighter.

Horn, Tom, was born in Missouri in 1860 and was hanged in 1903 for the killing of fourteen-year-old Willie Nickell, a crime for which some people to this day believe Horn was innocent, and of which he was acquitted in a modern day re-trial held in Cheyenne during the 1990s.

Houston, Pam, is a licensed fishing guide and accomplished horsewoman, as well as a writer of short stories and essays.

Hughes, Mack, earned his living as a working cowboy on his father's ranch and on several other early New Mexico ranches.

Hughes, William Patten "Pat," was the father of Mack and a New Mexico cowboy and rancher.

Irvine, Van, is a working cowboy.

Irving, Washington, was a New York writer and diplomat who made a journey to the West in the 1830s, which he chronicled in *The Tour of the Prairies*.

Irwin, Charles, was a Wyoming rancher, rodeo stock contractor, and wild west show producer during the late nineteenth and early twentieth centuries. Irwin owned Steamboat for most of the horse's life.

Isaacs, Chris, is a modern-day Arizona working cowboy and cowboy poet.

Isabell, Branch, was a Texas trail driver during the mid- to late 1800s.

Jacobs, John G., was a Texas cowboy and trail driver during the trails' heyday in the mid- to late 1800s.

Jakes, John, is a writer known for his multi-volume family sagas.

James, Will, was an early cowboy artist and writer who wrote and illustrated many classic western books including *Smoky: The Story of a Cow Pony*.

Johnson, Dorothy M., was a western author who wrote extensively about the Plains Indians.

Kelly, Bill, is a western historian and writer.

Kelton, Elmer, is a western writer.

Kennon, Bob, was a cowboy, rancher, forest ranger, stock inspector, and a deputy sheriff. He went up the trail in 1896 from Old Mexico to Montana, where he spent the rest of his days.

King, Richard, started out as a riverboat captain before founding the vast King Ranch in Texas. By the time he died in 1885, King's land holdings totaled over half a million acres.

Kiskaddon, Bruce, was a noted cowboy poet and began his ranch life in 1898 in the Picket Wire district of southern Colorado, in the Purgatory River country.

Knox, Ross, is a cowboy poet.

LaJeunesse, Lan, is a PRCA World Champion Bareback Bronc rider from Morgan, Utah.

Lambert, Cody, is a champion PRCA and PBR bull rider.

L'Amour, Louis, was the hugely popular author of western novels.

Love, Clara, was a turn-of-the-century writer.

Lucchese, Cosimo, is a well-known Master Boot Maker from Texas.

Mahan, Larry, is a six-time World Champion All-Around Cowboy who now lives in Texas.

Markus, Kurt, is a writer and photographer.

Marrin, Albert, is a native New Yorker who writes young adult nonfiction, including several histories of the Americas.

McCann, Barney, was the cook on an 1882 trail drive from Texas to Dodge City and then on to Montana.

McCauley, James Emmitt, was a cowpuncher during the early part of the twentieth century. McCauley had to retire from cowboy work at age thirty because of injuries suffered on the job.

McCoy, Cord, is an IPRA cowboy from Oklahoma. McCoy recently started up his own cattle outfit.

McCumber, David, is a journalist who chronicled his year as a ranch hand in *The Cowboy Way*.

McDowell, Bart, rode with cowboys and cowboyed himself during his younger years on his family's Mexican ranches. McDowell was a third generation cowboy-rancher until he left to become a writer.

McDowell, Caswell, was a cowboy and rancher.

McGuane, Thomas, is a best-selling author, Yale graduate, and owner of the Raw Deal Ranch in McLeod, Montana.

McMurtry, Larry, is a Texas-based western historian, author, and scriptwriter who is intimately acquainted with the cowboy way during both modern and olden times. He is the author of the classic cowboy tale, *Lonesome Dove*, which many have called The Great American Novel.

McNulta, Mr., was a Texas cattle drover in the late 1800s.

Michener, James A., was a Pulitzer-Prize winning author known for his voluminous research.

Mitchell, Waddie, is one of the country's best-known cowboy poets and western performers. He has been a working cowboy for nearly 26 years and is one of the co-founders of the Elko Cowboy Poetry Gathering.

Mix, Tom, was a popular star of old-time western movies.

Mizell, Morgan Bonaparte (Bone), was born in 1863 in the Horse Creek settlement in Manatee County, Florida. Depicted as "the Cracker Cowboy" in one of Frederic Remington's paintings, Bone was a colorful Florida cowboy or cow hunter during the late 1800s.

Montana, Gladiola, is a cowgirl chronicler and compiler of cowgirl logic and sayings as well as the writer of other humorous and commonsensical books on a variety of topics.

Mora, Jo, was a legendary early California cowpuncher or *vaquero*.

Morris, George Pope, was a journalist and poet.

Mullins, Jesse, is the editor of *American Cowboy* magazine, a writer, and a full-time advocate of the cowboy way of life.

Murphey, Michael Martin, is a popular western performer and songwriter who instituted Telluride, Colorado's West Fest. His best-known song is *Wildfire*. Murphey owns a horse and cattle operation, the Rocking 3M Brand Ranching Company, in Taos, Red River, and Jal, New Mexico.

Murray, Ty, has won the PRCA's World Champion All-Around Cowboy buckle a record seven times and went on to help found the Professional Bull Riders Association (PBR). He owns a cattle ranch in Henrietta, Texas.

Nance, Berta Hart, was a Texas author.

Newton, Bobby, is the ex-director of the Academy of Western Artists and also the publisher of *Rope Burns*, a cowboy newspaper.

Nordhoff, Charles, was an American journalist and author.

Nuce, Ted, is a champion bull rider.

Oakley, Annie, was a sharpshooter who starred in Buffalo Bill's Wild West show. Assisted by her husband, Frank Butler, part of her act was to shoot a dime out of his hand or a cigarette out of his mouth.

O'Connor, Sandra Day, is a Supreme Court Justice of the United States, who grew up cowboying on the family's Lazy B Ranch on the Arizona-New Mexico state line.

O'Malley, D. J., was a cowboy, poet, and writer.

Overcast, Ken, cowboys today in Montana.

Parkman, Francis, was an American historian, famed for his account of his journey along the Oregon Trail in the 1840s.

Patterson, Jim, is a modern-day Texas cowboy.

Perry, Jim, was cowboy, cook, and fiddler for the famed XIT Ranch in Texas.

Pickett, Dee, was the 1984 PRCA World Champion All-Around Cowboy.

Ponting, Tom Candy, traveled with Washington Malone during 1852 from Christian County, Illinois, to Texas where they bought a herd of steers. The two then drove their herd to Illinois to overwinter before continuing onward the following spring to New York.

Potter, Jack, was a trail driver from Kenton, Oklahoma.

Putney, "Put," was one of the last Texas Rangers to go head to head with the outlaws of the late nineteenth century. Putney frowned on modern-day methods of apprehending criminals, preferring to shoot first and ask questions later.

Reagan, Ronald, traveled to Hollywood from the Midwest. He became an actor, president of the Screen Actors Guild, governor of California, and then was twice elected President of the United States. Reagan always considered himself a cowboy at heart and spent his free time and his retirement years at his California ranch.

Remington, Frederic, was an illustrator who traveled west before the turn of the century to ride with cowboys, observe Native Americans, and visit the U.S. Cavalry. His paintings, drawings, and sculptures are today highly coveted by Western aficionados, galleries, and museums.

Reynolds, Ralph, a.k.a. The Luna Kid, was born, raised, and cowboyed in New Mexico.

Roderus, Frank, is an award-winning author of western fiction.

Rogers, Roy, was named Leonard Slye before he attained stardom. When he became Roy Rogers he often rode with his real wife, Dale Evans, and comic sidekick Pat Brady. Roy, whose horse was named Trigger, was known as the "King of the Cowboys." Rogers gained fame in movies and in his own TV series.

Rogers, Will, an Oklahoma cowboy of Native American heritage, was America's most popular humorist during the 1920s. Rogers not only became the country's biggest box office movie star, he was also its most widely read newspaper columnist.

Roosevelt, Theodore, was a cowboy, hunter, conservationist, and two-time President of the U.S. Born sickly, when he was old enough to travel to the West he became a cowboy, acquired a ranch, and credited this lifestyle to improving his vigor and health.

Rosa, Joseph G., is an English author of the definitive biography of Wild Bill Hickok, who also writes on many Old West subjects.

Russell, Andy, is a former bronc buster and mountain man.

Russell, Charles M., was a noted cowboy artist, sculptor and writer who had traveled as a young man from his St. Louis, Missouri, home to the Judith Mountains in Montana where he lived out the remainder of his life.

Rust, C. H., was a Texas cowboy and cattle drover during the time of the great trail drives.

Santos, Kendra, is the editor of *Pro Bull Rider* magazine and is the rodeo columnist for *American Cowboy* magazine

Saunders, George W., was for fifty years a Texas trail driver during the cattle-driving heyday.

Siringo, Charles, wrote about cowboy life during the early years of the Texas cattle industry.

Sitting Bull, was a famous medicine man and leader of the Hunkpapa band of the Teton Sioux Indians.

Smedley, Agnes, as a young woman in the early twentieth century, rode a horse alone, with a gun slung at her side, through the deserts of the Southwest.

Smyth, Bernie, was an Australian all-around cowboy who immigrated to Canada in 1990 to compete in North American rodeos.

Soule, John Babson, was a nineteenth-century Indiana journalist, who inspired newspaperman Horace Greeley to write "To Aspiring Young Men." Soule, however, did not get around to publishing his famous advice until ten years after Greeley's *New York Tribune* editorial appeared in print.

Sparks, Ronny, is a Wrangler World Bullfight Tour Champion.

Steagall, Red, is a cowboy poet, songwriter, and performer who started out as a working cowboy.

Stewart, Bronco Sam, was one of the finest horseback riders and cowboys the West has ever known, yet many of Sam's exploits have not survived to the present day. Stewart believed gossipmongers regarding his wife's infidelity and shot both her and himself.

Streeter, Floyd B., was an American historian.

Taylor, L. D., was born in San Antonio, Texas, and in 1869 drove a herd north from Texas to Abilene, Kansas, along the Chisholm Trail.

Tibbs, Casey, was a legendary rodeo roughstock champion of the 1940s and 1950s. Tibbs, who came from South Dakota, seven times garnered World Champion Saddle Bronc Rider accolades from the PRCA.

Tomac, Steve, has been a state senator in North Dakota, and also is a PRCA rodeo clown or bullfighter.

Twain, Mark, was the pen name of Samuel Clemons. The famed humorist was once a correspondent for the Virginia City, Nevada, *Territorial Enterprise*.

Tyson, Ian, is an Alberta rancher, cutting horse trainer and breeder, and legendary cowboy songwriter. He was formerly half of the Ian and Sylvia folk group of the 1960s. Tyson wrote the hit song, "Someday Soon," made famous by Judy Collins.

Van Cleve, Spike, was a third generation Montanan who grew up under the Crazy Mountains in the state's Melville country. Van Cleve graduated from Harvard with a literature degree but went home to Montana. He became a beloved writer and chronicler of the cowboy way of life.

Wayne, John, was raised in Iowa, the Mojave Desert, and Glendale, California. He began his career as a Hollywood prop man and worked his way to the top of the Hollywood star system. Best known for a string of much-loved westerns, Wayne owned a vast Arizona cattle ranch with his partner, Louis Johnson, and cowboyed there during his free time. He was born Marion Morrison.

Webb, Walter Prescott, was a Texas historian and author.

Whitfield, Fred, is a cowboy who earned the title of PRCA World Champion All-Around Cowboy for his calf-roping prowess.

Wilhite, George was a rodeo cowboy and a rodeo clown/bullfighter before becoming a fiction writer.

Williams, Speed, is a "header" on a PRCA World Champion Roping team.

Wister, Owen, was a writer and author of the beloved 1902 Western novel *The Virginian*. Wister was himself a cowboy.

Bibliography

Abbot, Edward C. (Teddy Blue), and Helena H. Smith
We Pointed Them North: Recollections of a Cowpuncher
(1939)

Adams, Andy
The Log of a Cowboy: A Narrative of the Old Trail Days
(1903)

Adams, Ramon F.
Cowboy Lingo (1936)

Arnold, Darrell and Richard Farnsworth
The Cowboy Kind (2001)

Axelrod, Alan (editor)
Ranching Traditions (1989)

Beery, Gladys B.
Sinners & Saints (1994)

Bender, Texas Bix
Don't Squat With Yer Spurs On (1992)

Black, Baxter
Cactus Tracks and Cowboy Philosophy (1997)

Blasingame, Ike
Dakota Cowboy: My Life in the Old Days (1964)

Botkin, B. A. (editor)
A Treasury of Western Folklore (1975)

Bowen, Ezra (editor)
The Cowboys (1973)

Bowman, R. Lewis
Bumfuzzled (1992)
Bumfuzzled, Too (2001)

Brannaman, Buck
The Faraway Horses (2001)

Branch, Edward Douglas
The Cowboy and His Interpreters (1926)

Brown, Dee
Trail Driving Days (1952)

Burk, Martha Canary (Calamity Jane)
Life and Adventures of Calamity Jane, by Herself (N.d.)

Carlson, Chip
Tom Horn: The Definitive History of the Notorious Wyoming Stock Detective (1991)

Cather, Willa
O Pioneers! (1913)

Chapman, Arthur
Out Where the West Begins (1917)

Clay, John Randolph
My Life on the Range (1924)

Clayton, Lawrence (editor)
Horsing Around: Contemporary Cowboy Humor (1999)

Coplon, Jeff
Gold Buckle: The Grand Obsession of Rodeo Bull Riders (1995)

Craze, Sophia
Charles Russell (1989)
Frederic Remington (1999)

Dary, Dave
Cowboy Culture: A Saga of Five Centuries (1989)

Davis, Tom, as told to Marilyn Ross
Be Tough or Be Gone: The Adventures of a Modern Day Cowboy (1984)

Dobie, J. Frank
A Vaquero of the Brush Country (1929)

Dobie, J. Frank, Mody C. Boatright, Harry H. Ransom (editors)
Mustangs and Cow Horses (1940)

Durham, Marilyn
Dutch Uncle (1973)

Erickson, John R.
LZ Cowboy: A Cowboy's Journal 1979–81 (1996)

Evans, Clay Bonnyman
I See by Your Outfit: Becoming a Cowboy a Century Too Late (1999)

Evans, Nicholas
The Horse Whisperer (1995)

Forbis, William H.
The Cowboys (The Old West Series) (1978)

Grey, Zane
The Riders of the Purple Sage (1912)

Editors of Guns and Ammo Magazine
Guns and the Gunfighters (1975)

Haley, J. Evetts
Charles Goodnight: Cowman and Plainsman (1949)

Hillerman, Tony
The Best of the West: An Anthology of Classic Writing from the American West (1991)

Houston, Pam
Cowboys Are My Weakness (1992)

Hughes, Stella
Hashknife Cowboy: Recollections of Mack Hughes (1984)

Hunter, J. Marvin (editor)
The Trail Drivers of Texas (1925)

Jakes, John
The Lawless (1978)

James, Will
The American Cowboy (1942)

Kennon, Bob, as told to Ramon F. Adams
From the Pecos to the Powder: A Cowboy's Autobiography (1965)

King, Frank M.
Longhorn Trail Drivers: Being a True Story of the Cattle Drives of Long Ago (1940)

L'Amour, Louis
The Rustlers of West Fork (1951)

Love, Nat
The Life and Adventures of Nat Love (1907)

Marrin, Albert
Cowboys, Indians and Gunfighters (1993)

May, Stephen J.
  Zane Grey, Romancing the West (1997)

McCauley, James Emmitt
  A Stove-Up Cowboy's Story (1965)

McCumber, David
  The Cowboy Way: Seasons of a Montana Ranch (2000)

McDowell, Bart
  The American Cowboy in Life and Legend (1972)

McGuane, Thomas
  Some Horses (1999)

McMurtry, Larry
  Lonesome Dove (1985)
  Streets of Laredo (1993)

Michener, James A.
  Centennial (1974)

Montana, Gladiola
  Never Ask a Man the Size of His Spread: A Cowgirl's Guide to Life (1993)

Moulton, Candy Vyvey, and Flossie Moulton
  Steamboat, Legendary Bucking Horse: His Life and Times and the Cowboys Who Tried to Tame Him (1992)

Murray, Ty, and Kendra Santos
  Roughstock: The Mud, the Blood, and the Beer (2001)

Nelson, Kendall
Gathering Remnants: A Tribute to the Working Cowboy
(2001)

O'Connor, Sandra Day, and H. Alan Day
*Lazy B: Growing up on a Cattle Ranch in the American
Southwest* (2002)

O'Malley, D. J.
*Reminiscences and Poems of Early Montana and the
Cattle Range* (1934)

Parkman, Jr, Francis
The Oregon Trail (1849)

Pattie, Jane
John Wayne: There Rode a Legend (2000)

Philips, Shine
Big Spring: The Casual Biography of a Prairie Town
(1942)

Reynolds, Ralph
Growing Up Cowboy: Confessions of a Luna Kid (1991)

Roosevelt, Theodore
Theodore Roosevelt: An Autobiography (1913)
Hunting Trips of a Ranchman (1885)
Ranch Life and the Hunting Trail (1888)

Rosa, Joseph
Age of the Gunfighter: Men and Weapons of the Frontier 1840–1900 (1993)

Russell, Andy
The Canadian Cowboy: Stories of Cows, Cowboys, and Cayuses (1993)

Russell, Charles M
Charlie Russell Journal (1997)
Trails Plowed Under (1927)

Santos, Kendra
Ring of Fire: The Guts and Glory of the Professional Bull Riding Tour (2000)

Siringo, Charles
A Texas Cowboy, or Fifteen Years on the Hurricane Deck of a Spanish Pony (1888)

Soule, Gardner
The Long Trail (1976)

Steagall, Red
Ride for the Brand (2000)

Streeter, Floyd B
The Kaw: The Heart of a Nation (1941)
Prairie Trails and Cow Towns (1936)

Tinsley, Jim Bob
Florida Cow Hunter: The Life and Times of Bone Mizell
(1990)

Twain, Mark
Autobiography (1871)
Roughing It (1872)

Van Cleve, Spike
Forty Years Gatherin's (1977)

Webb, Walter Prescott
The Great Plains (1931)

Weston, Jack
The Real American Cowboy (1985)

Wister, Owen
The Virginian (1902)

Wooden, Wayne S., and Gavin Ehringer
Rodeo in America: Wranglers, Roughstock, and Paydirt
(1996)

Index

A

Abbott, E. C. "Teddy Blue," 52, 61, 64, 76, 97, 189

Adams, Andy, 79, 100, 102, 125, 151, 155, 186

Adams, Ramon F., 28, 33, 79, 91, 141, 168

Allen, Guy, 62

Allen, James, 62

Allen, Rex, 61, 77, 78, 194

Anonymous, 14, 26, 74, 77, 107, 110, 115, 137, 138, 144, 152, 153, 171, 183, 191, 193, 194

Arnold, Darrell, 98

Autry, Gene, 37, 44, 66, 67

B

Baker, Nathan A., 144

Bean, Roy, 148

Beasley, Parry, 82

Beaver, Joe, 172

Bender, Texas Bix, 36, 109, 122

Billy the Kid, 139

Black, Baxter, 55, 88, 97, 105, 109, 113, 118, 177

Blasingame, Ike, 127

Blocker, Ab, 80

Bower, B. M., 126

Bowman, R. Lewis, 30, 47, 58, 71, 72, 102, 113, 118

Boxleitner, Bruce, 65

Branch, Edward Douglas, 18, 51

Brand, Max, 133

Brannaman, Buck, 58, 102, 165

Brown, Freckles, 171

Brown, J. P. S., 63

Brummett, Curt, 118, 199, 202

Burrows, G. D., 70

C

Calamity Jane, 86

Cameron, Craig, 165

Cather, Willa, 4

Chapman, Arthur, 5, 195

Cheyenne Daily Leader, 144, 183

Christian, Jim, 89

Clanton, Billy, 159
Clark, Walter Van
    Tilburg, 192
Clay, John Randolph,
    60
Code of the West, 35
Cody, Buffalo Bill,
    197, 198
Coleman, Evans, 60
Colt six-shooter, 129,
    131
Cowboy greeting, 90
Cowboy sayings, 9,
    27, 28, 30, 36, 40,
    41, 43, 45, 53, 71,
    82, 95, 104, 105,
    107, 115, 121,
    122, 136, 141,
    153, 165, 168,
    169
Cowboy's Code, 36,
    37
Cowboy's Philosophy,
    36
Cowboy songs, 6, 17,
    31, 81, 127, 132,
    147, 160, 183,
    184

Cox, Ken "Butch,"
    161, 177
Cunninghame
    Graham, R. B., 25

D

Dalton, Bob, 160
Danks, Clayton, 168
Dary, Dave, 121, 199
Davis, Tom, 39, 109,
    113, 123
Day, H. C., 15
Dightman, Myrtis, 175
Dobie, J. Frank, 46,
    111, 117
Dodge City, Kansas,
    cowboy names
    for, 9, 11
Drover slang, 28, 152,
    156
Drover songs, 127
Duffy, Dann, 202
Durham, Marilyn, 157

E

Earp, Wyatt, 137, 159
Eastwood, Clint, 49,
    66, 91

Ehringer, Gavin,
    163
Elliott, Sam, 65
Ellsworth Reporter, 133
Erickson, John R., 45,
    53, 64, 91, 93,
    191, 193
Estelman, Loren D.,
    17
Etbauer, Billy, 170
Etling, K. T., 179
Evans, Clay
    Bonnyman, 9, 20
Evans, Dale, 85
Evans, Nicholas, 99

F

*Finney County
    Democrat,* 75
Flood, Jim, 13, 95
Forbis, William H.,
    124, 142
Ford, John, 64, 67
Forrest, Quince,
    157
Frantz, Joe B., 198
Frost, Kellie, 173
Frost, Lane, 173

G

Garrett, Pat, 139
Gee, Mickey, 163
Gibson, Hoot, 69
"Git Along Little
    Dogies," 127
"Gitto," 143
Goodnight, Charles,
    18, 39, 44, 106,
    117, 121, 186
Grey, Zane, 4, 24, 76,
    88, 126, 138, 149
Growney, John, 98,
    175

H

Hanson, Royce,
    117
Hargo, Dwayne, 45
Harte, Bret, 142
Hedeman, Tuff, 173
Hickok, Wild Bill,
    132, 134, 135,
    136, 137, 214
Hickox, Hub, 155
Higley, Brewster, 17
Holliday, Doc, 137,
    159

Horn, Tom, 145
Houston, Pam, 4, 82
Hughes, Mack, 106,
    107, 112
Hughes, Pat, 58, 60
Hunt, Jap, 149

I

Irvine, Van, 83
Irving, Washington,
    151
Irwin Brothers, 166,
    216
Irwin, Charles, 184
Isaacs, Chris, 39
Isabell, Branch, 79

J

Jacobs, John G.,
    186
Jakes, John, 26, 134,
    148, 156
James, Will, 3, 19, 26,
    43, 49, 61, 108,
    141, 181
Jim (cowboy), 144
Johnson, Dorothy M.,
    21

K

Kansas City Journal,
    147
Kelly, Bill, 139
Kelton, Elmer, 16
Kennon, Bob, 7, 63,
    145, 200
King, Frank, 110
King, Richard, 15
Kiskaddon, Bruce,
    88
Knox, Ross, 81

L

LaJeunesse, Lan,
    164
Lambert, Cody, 47
L'Amour, Louis, 6, 90,
    140, 201
*London Daily
    Telegraph,* 154
"The Lone Ranger's
    Creed," 37
Love, Clara M., 116
Love, Nat, 24, 111,
    135
Lucchese, Cosimo,
    192

M

Mahan, Larry, 172

Mannes, Marya, 192

Markus, Kurt, 57, 73

Marrin, Albert, 68, 75, 115, 197

McCann, Barney, 155

McCauley, James Emmit, 62

McCoy, Cord, 116

McCumber, David, 94, 200

McDowell, Bart, 122

McDowell, Caswell, 94

McGuane, Thomas, 69, 99

McMurtry, Larry, 56, 68, 136, 149

McNulta, Mr., 12, 132

Michener, James A., 114, 125

Miller, Mike, 59, 87

Mitchell, Waddie, 68, 199

Mix, Tom, 67, 69, 202

Mizell, Bone, 29, 119, 148, 150, 185

Montana, Gladiola, 35, 81, 83, 108

Mora, Jo, 106

Morris, George Pope, 5

Mullins, Jesse, 41, 51, 79

Murray, Ty, 44, 62, 93, 163, 169, 172, 173

Murphey, Michael Martin, 25, 111

N

Nance, Berta Hart, 13

Newton, Bobby, 191

Nordhoff, Charles, 164

Nuce, Ted, 175

O

Oakley, Annie, 87

"O Bury Me Not on the Lone Prairie," 183

O'Connor, Sandra Day, 15, 89, 98

"The Old Chisholm Trail," 31

O'Malley, D. J., 77

Overcast, Ken, 198

P

Parkman, Francis H., xi

Patterson, Jim, 116

Perry, Jim, 170, 171

Philips, Shine, 87

Pickett, Dee, 164

Ponting, Tom, 21

Potter, Jack, 123

Putney, "Put", 71, 131, 150

R

Ray, Dusty, 16

Reagan, Ronald, 65

Remington, Frederic, 1, 72

Reynolds, Ralph, 53, 59, 120

Rodeo call, 45

Roderus, Frank, 56

Rogers, Roy, 184, 201

Rogers, Will, 98, 145, 184, 190
Roosevelt, Theodore, 3, 13, 18, 37, 43, 52, 104, 120, 143, 154, 188, 190, 194
Rosa, Joseph G., 9
Russell, Andy, 55, 73, 112, 131, 135
Russell, Charles M., 7, 22, 52, 71, 83, 89, 97, 110, 181, 186, 189, 197
Rust, C. H., 11

S
Santos, Kendra, 175, 178
Saunders, George W., 85
Sign on prairie cabin door, 90
Siringo, Charles, 70
Sitting Bull, 86
Smedley, Agnes, 85
Smyth, Bernie, 161

Soule, John Babson, 5
Sparks, Ronny, 176
Steagall, Red, 40, 100, 185
Steamboat, 166, 168, 184
Stewart, Bronco Sam, 143
Streeter, Floyd B., 19, 151
"Streets of Laredo," 147

T
Taylor, L. D., 22
Texas Livestock Journal, 40
Texas Ranger Creed, 140
Tibbs, Casey, 166, 201
Tomac, Steve, 176
Topeka Daily Commonwealth, 157
"The Trail to Mexico," 6

Tucson, Arizona, cowboy name for, 9
Twain, Mark, 12, 152
Tyson, Ian, 73

V
Van Cleve, Spike, 7, 146

W
Wayne, John, 1, 33, 42, 66, 78, 93, 100
Webb, Walter Prescott, 74
Whitfield, Fred, 170, 171
Wilhite, George, 176
Williams, Speed, 169
Winchester rifle, 129
Wister, Owen, 158, 188, 190

Y
The Yankton Press and Dakotaian, 136
Young, John, 160